Twayne's United States Authors Series

Sylvia E. Bowman, *Editor*

INDIANA UNIVERSITY

James T. Farrell

JAMES T. FARRELL

By EDGAR M. BRANCH
Miami University

 185

Twayne Publishers, Inc. :: New York

To Marian and Toddy

Preface

James T. Farrell's first commercially published story appeared forty years ago in 1929. Recently, he brought out his thirty-fifth volume of fiction and his forty-fourth book. Other volumes are completed in manuscript or are in progress. His many fictions cohere into a unifed and detailed interpretation of modern American experience. Despite varying estimates of his stature as artist, it is generally conceded that he is a leading figure in the tradition of American Realism. Among his novels, *Studs Lonigan* and the O'Neill-O'Flaherty pentalogy are monumental achievements of this century.

Yet in this age when everything is published and much is acclaimed, no book before this one has been devoted to Farrell or his work. Most of his fiction is out of print; the Modern Library recently dropped *Studs Lonigan*. Nor have the critics turned his way. To be sure, Farrell has had a number of even-handed interpreters and some sympathetic ones. But many others have dismissed him out of hand. Some critics, in apologetic tones, have focused less on Farrell's writing than on his "case." The hostility or condescension of still others has become legendary. As a result, his writing has not been examined with care.

This book is a reasonably inclusive account of Farrell's writings. It gives priority to his fiction, and specifically to the twenty-two novels published to date, because they are of first importance in his art. With a few exceptions, the treatment is chronological, as in the successive chapters on Farrell's three completed series about Studs Lonigan, the O'Neills and the O'Flahertys, and Bernard Carr. But, as a matter of practicability, the scattered individual novels outside the series are considered together, as are the more than two hundred tales written over four decades. The enormous volume of the fiction and the space restrictions of this book have combined to prevent a detailed examination of Farrell's nonfiction, including his literary criticism, recently ably discussed by William J. Lynch. Nor was it possible to expand on Farrell's participation in the ideological

Preface

debates and the political currents of his times. Nevertheless, Chapter 1 includes a relatively full outline of Farrell's early experience—through the mid-1930's—because that experience was basic to most of his completed fiction.

I have relied heavily upon Farrell's letters and unpublished manuscripts, and I wish to thank Mr. Farrell for giving me access to his papers at the University of Pennsylvania Library. I wish especially to thank Mrs. Neda M. Westlake, Mr. Lyman W. Riley, and Mrs. Jean F. Jones who helped me find my way through the Farrell Collection there, and Mr. James Henle and Miss Evelyn Shrifte of Vanguard Press who have been unfailingly helpful. Also I wish to thank Mr. Farrell and his friends for answering my questions.

I am grateful to the Faculty Research Committee and the Administration of Miami University for grants of money over the past few years. In particular I wish to thank Mr. John D. Millett and Mr. Spiro Peterson, both of whom helped make available to me the free time needed for this work. Finally, because my wife Mary Jo and my daughters Sydney and Marian found pleasure in sharing an initial interest of mine that has snowballed beyond all expectations, I am just generally thankful.

Edgar M. Branch

Miami University
Oxford, Ohio

Contents

Acknowledgments

I am grateful to James T. Farrell for permission to quote from his letters and other unpublished material, to James Henle for permission to quote from his letters, and to Dorothy Pound for permission to quote from Ezra Pound's letters. I wish to thank the following publishers for permission to quote from the works listed:

Vanguard Press, Inc.: *The Short Stories of James T. Farrell.* Copyright 1934, 1937, 1961, 1964, by James T. Farrell. *No Star Is Lost* by James T. Farrell. Copyright 1938, 1965, by James T. Farrell.

Fleet Press Corporation: *The Collected Poems of James T. Farrell,* copyright © James T. Farrell Fleet Press Corporation.

Some material in this book is reprinted or adapted from portions of my earlier writings on James T. Farrell. I wish to thank the publishers listed below for permission to make use of the indicated publications:

Mr. William B. Thorsen for: "James T. Farrell's *Studs Lonigan*" and "American Writer in the Twenties: James T. Farrell and the University of Chicago," *American Book Collector,* XI (Summer, 1961), copyright 1961 William B. Thorsen; "James T. Farrell," *American Book Collector,* XVI (September, 1965), copyright 1965 William B. Thorsen.

Kent State University Press for: "Freedom and Determinism in James T. Farrell's Fiction," *Essays on Determinism in American Literature,* ed. Sydney J. Krause, 1964, copyright © 1964 Kent State University and James T. Farrell.

National Council of Teachers of English for: "Studs Lonigan: Symbolism and Theme," *College English,* XXIII (December, 1961), copyright © 1961 National Council of Teachers of English.

University of Kansas City for: "Destiny, Culture, and Technique: *Studs Lonigan,*" *University of Kansas City Review,* XXIX (December, 1962), copyright © 1962 University of Kansas City.

University of Minnesota Press for: *James T. Farrell,* 1963, copyright © 1963, University of Minnesota.

Chronology

1904   James Thomas Farrell born February 27 in Chicago, Illinois, to Mary Daly Farrell and James Francis Farrell. Second of six children who lived to adulthood: William Earl, James, Helen, Joseph, John, Mary.

1907   Taken to live with his grandparents, John and Julia Brown Daly, Chicago.

1910   Grandfather John Daly dies, December.

1911   Aunt Elizabeth (Bessie) Daly dies, May. Enters first grade at Corpus Christi Parochial Grammar School.

1915   Moves May 1 with the Dalys into the neighborhood depicted in first two volumes of *Studs Lonigan;* enters fourth grade at St. Anselm's Parochial Grammar School.

1919   Enters St. Cyril High School (now Mount Carmel).

1920   First works as a call clerk for express company, June-August.

1921   Publishes compositions in St. Cyril *Oriflamme* for two years, beginning with "Danny's Uncle" in February, 1921.

1923   Graduates from St. Cyril High School. Begins full-time work at express company in July and continues until March, 1925. Father dies, November.

1924   Takes one semester, beginning in September, as pre-law student at De Paul University night school.

1925   Begins work as service-station attendant, March. Matriculates in June at University of Chicago; continues through Spring Quarter, 1926.

1926   Resumes studies at University of Chicago in October; continues through Winter Quarter, 1927.

1927   Takes Professor Linn's English 210, Advanced English Composition, Winter Quarter. Decides to be a writer, March. Hitchhikes in July to New York City, where he works as clerk and salesman, reads widely, writes.

1928   Returns to Chicago in January, completes several stories, meets Dorothy Butler. Hitchhikes to Indianapolis and returns, early summer. Takes two composition classes, second summer term at University of Chicago. Moves southeast into Studs's neighborhood depicted in *Judgment Day*.

1929   Works as reporter for Chicago *Herald Examiner*. Writes "Studs" in spring. Enrolls for Spring Quarter, his last; takes Professor Linn's English 211, Advanced English Composition. "Slob," his first published tale, appears in *Blues* (June). Makes second New York trip in August; returns to Chicago, October.

1930   "Studs" published in *This Quarter* (July-August-September).

1931   Marries Dorothy Patricia Butler April 13; leaves for Paris later in April. Vanguard Press accepts *Young Lonigan*, June. Grandmother Julia Brown Daly dies October 2.

1932   Returns from Paris in April; takes up residence in New York. *Young Lonigan* published April 21. "Helen, I Love You" in *American Mercury* (July).

1933   *Gas-House McGinty*, February 16. First goes to Yaddo in August; stays there intermittently until August, 1935.

1934   *The Young Manhood of Studs Lonigan*, January 30. *Calico Shoes and Other Stories*, September 28.

1935   Joins League of American Writers in April. *Judgment Day*, April 27. Speaks on April 28 on "The Short Story" at American Writers' Congress. Separates from Dorothy Farrell in August. *Guillotine Party and Other Stories*, October 5. Rejects Hollywood scriptwriting offer. *Studs Lonigan: A Trilogy*, November 21.

1936   Wins $2,500 Guggenheim Fellowship for 1936-1937 in creative writing, March 30. *A Note on Literary Criticism*, May 20. Attends Democratic (June) and Republican (July) National Conventions; meets H. L. Mencken and Theodore Dreiser; later supports Socialist ticket. *A World I Never Made*, first Danny O'Neill novel, October 22. Gives speech denouncing Moscow Trials, December 18.

1937   Book of the Month Club Fellowship Award of $2,500 for *Studs Lonigan*, January. Wins censorship case concerning *A World I Never Made*, February. In Mexico, March to May, to observe the Commission of Inquiry for the American Committee for the Defense of Leon Trotsky; meets John Dewey. *Can All This Grandeur Perish? and Other*

Stories, May 6. Begins lecturing for fees. *The Short Stories of James T. Farrell*, September 28.

1938 In England, France, Ireland from May to August. *No Star Is Lost*, July 18.

1939 *Tommy Gallagher's Crusade*, October 6.

1940 Divorced from Dorothy Farrell in June. *Father and Son*, October 10.

1941 Marries Hortense Alden, January 12. Takes course in symbolic logic at New York University. Helps organize Civil Rights Defense Committee in July; later becomes chairman. *Ellen Rogers*, September 25. Spends two weeks in Hollywood as film writer, October. Elected to The National Institute of Arts and Letters, December 10.

1942 *$1,000 a Week and Other Stories*, March 30.

1943 *My Days of Anger*, October 25.

1944 *To Whom It May Concern and Other Stories*, May 25. Wins censorship case in Chicago, October.

1945 *The League of Frightened Philistines and Other Papers*, June 26.

1946 Mother dies, January. *Bernard Clare*, the first Bernard Carr novel, published May 13. "The Fate of Writing in America" published in June. *When Boyhood Dreams Come True*, November 14. December apartment fire destroys manuscripts.

1947 Member Workers' Defense Committee. *Literature and Morality*, June 27. *The Life Adventurous and Other Stories*, October 7.

1948 On Executive Committee, Workers Defense League. Wins Philadelphia censorship case concerning *Studs Lonigan* and *A World I Never Made* in May. Actively supports Socialist ticket, July to November. Member New York State Liberal Party, 1948-1958.

1949 *The Road Between*, March 23. Speaks on "Truth and Myth about America" at the Paris Conference for Mobilization for Peace, April. Wins Newberry Library Fellowship for work on *Yet Other Waters*.

1950 Chairman of Committee against Jim Crow in Military Training, January. *The Name Is Fogarty; Private Papers on Public Matters*, March 15. Speaks at Berlin Congress for Cultural Freedom; helps organize the International

Congress for Cultural Freedom, June. *An American Dream Girl*, October 27. Helps found the Fund for Intellectual Freedom, December.

1951 Separates from Hortense Farrell in July. *This Man and This Woman*, October 9. Trip to California, October-November, following illness.

1952 Participates in Paris Festival of the Arts (Congress for Cultural Freedom) in May; speaks at International Congress of the PEN Club, Nice, June. *Yet Other Waters*, October 20. Recuperates from abdominal operation, November-December.

1953 Chairman of Committee for Spanish Refugee Aid, May. *The Face of Time*, October 15. Makes sixth European trip.

1954 Speaks at International Congress of the PEN Club, Amsterdam, June. Lecture tour of Sweden and Denmark, September-October. *Reflections at Fifty and Other Essays*, November 17. Elected Chairman of the American Committee for Cultural Freedom, December 17.

1955 Divorces Hortense Farrell and remarries Dorothy Farrell, September. Re-elected Chairman of American Committee for Cultural Freedom. *French Girls Are Vicious and Other Stories*, December 9.

1956 Makes world lecture tour for American Committee for Cultural Freedom, April-August; visits Israel, June-August. *An Omnibus of Short Stories*, December 3.

1957 *A Dangerous Woman and Other Stories*, September 27. *My Baseball Diary*, November 13.

1958 *It Has Come to Pass*, November 14. Separates from Dorothy Farrell in September.

1959 *Dialogue on John Dewey* (Farrell a participant), October 10.

1960 Film *Studs Lonigan* released in July.

1961 *Boarding House Blues*, June 15. *Side Street and Other Stories*, September 15.

1962 *Sound of a City*, December 13.

1963 *The Silence of History*, his first book with Doubleday and first volume in *A Universe of Time* series, published February 15.

1964 *What Time Collects*, June 19.

1965 *The Collected Poems of James T. Farrell*, March 28.

1966 *Lonely for the Future*, January 14. *When Time Was Born*, September 15.
1967 *New Year's Eve / 1929*, November 20.
1968 *A Brand New Life*, June 28.
1969 *Judith*, May 1. In Paris and London, May. *Childhood Is Not Forever*, September 19.
1971 *Invisible Swords* and *Judith and Other Stories* planned for publication by Doubleday.

CHAPTER 1

"Of Plebeian Origin"

IN 1928, while he was still a college student, James T. Farrell began to conceive a life-plan for writing twenty-five volumes of fiction. These books were to be loosely integrated—"panels of one work," he wrote on August 27, 1934 to his friend Jack Kunitz. They would picture life in "connected social areas," first and basically in Chicago and then elsewhere. Including many characters, they would try to catch the human meaning of "social processes" or "social forces": the "potentialities of action . . . resident in human beings." Farrell expressed his intention to James Henle, his editor at Vanguard Press, in a letter of May 28, 1941: "What I want to do in this whole series of at least twenty-five books is to drive toward a feeling about life, a point of view, a thorough and exhaustive account of a way of life, a period, of endless and complicated tendencies pressing for action."

He published his twenty-fifth book of fiction in 1957, twenty-five years after his first. Behind him were the Studs Lonigan trilogy, the Danny O'Neill pentalogy, the Bernard Carr trilogy, three other novels, a novelette, ten collections of tales, and a play (with Hortense Alden Farrell), as well as six books of essays and criticism. The fiction recreates "connected social areas" through its range of characterization and its use of cultural details. Its geographical poles are Chicago and New York City, but other parts of America and Europe receive attention. A surprising number of memorable characters move about in their homes and neighborhoods during their leisure and working hours. They represent four generations, and their actions span half a century. They come from a wide variety of social, economic, professional, national, and ethnic groups. Revealing a steadfast purpose and unrelenting endeavor, Farrell has explored,

15

with a complexity not generally recognized, a representative segment of America; and, in doing so, he has established his personal style and his mode of Realism.

Since 1957 he has added other "panels." *Judith* (1969) is his twenty-second novel, his thirty-fifth volume of fiction, and his forty-fourth book. His present hope, time permitting, is to expand his lifework to include at least fifty-eight books of fiction. Toward that goal he is making steady progress as he continues to bring out portions of his massive new series, *A Universe of Time.*

This prolific author once suggested in a letter of August 25, 1945, to J. Donald Adams, some of the problems that an "American writer of plebeian origin"—a man like himself—is faced with in his youth:

He is brought up on banalities, commonplaces, formal religious fanaticism, spiritual emptiness, an authoritative educational system (it is less so now than it was in my day), Horatio Algerism and so on. The success he is told about achieving is infrequently [as] possible as it was in the past. . . . He usually has to work his own way through college, and in doing so, he learns that most of the talk about education is not meant except in the sense of where will it get you. He sees things from the outside, not the inside. And seeing them from the outside, he not only acquires a different point of view than earlier writers like Emerson and Henry James, but he also knows that he can't get inside except by deforming his own nature, and his impulses. . . . He doesn't begin with a consciousness of the complications which are the source material of writers in a more sophisticated culture, and he doesn't absorb forms and traditions. His subject matter is his own world around him, and from that he gradually expands. . . . The feelings of alienation he meets sometimes make him hardened, stubborn and resistant. He spends his youth in struggling to get what a son of Groton acquires as if by natural right.

I *Ancestry and Boyhood*

Farrell was no son of Groton. He was born February 27, 1904, in Chicago, where he lived until April, 1931, except for eight months spent in New York City during the late 1920's. His mother was Mary Daly Farrell, a native of Chicago, a domestic servant before her marriage, and a devout Catholic until her death in 1946. Her parents were John and Julia Brown Daly of County Westmeath in the Irish Midlands where they had been neighbors and had shared a background of poverty. During the Civil War they came to America a few months apart and began married life in Brooklyn. By 1871, after a brief stay in Green Bay, Wisconsin, they were settled in Chicago and were raising a growing family on John's meager earnings as a teamster. Eventually they had seven children, five of whom lived past childhood: Richard Thomas, Mary, Ella, William, and Elizabeth. None of the children went to high school, for the family was poor. In a recent untitled manuscript, Farrell imagines his grandfather as "up before dawn in the darkness of winter mornings, and out with the men and the horses. His face was marked by the winds of many winters that came stinging cold off Lake Michigan." The grandparents remained illiterate and always kept their simple peasant ways. They never really understood America— just as the peppery old Julia could not fathom the mysteries of the White Sox baseball games she saw with her grandson James.

Farrell's paternal grandfather was James Farrell of Tipperary who emigrated to New Orleans and became an overseer of slaves. During the Civil War, Farrell believes, he enlisted as a foot soldier in the Louisiana Tigers, and after the war he lived in Kentucky, married, and became a sewer sweeper. He moved to Chicago where, after the birth of a son, his wife died and he remarried. His son was Farrell's father, James Francis ("Big Jim"). Farrell believes that his father taught himself to read and to write and that for a time he went to St. Mary's School in Des Plaines, Illinois. Like John Daly, James Francis Farrell became a Chicago teamster. For much of his life he worked on the wagons, although around 1900 he tried to start his own saloon—a business man for two weeks—and, before he died in 1923, he had been promoted to scripper and then wagon dispatcher for the Railway Express Agency. Farrell remembers him as a proud, independent, hot-tempered man. A tall, rugged fighter, Big Jim once beat up a gangster; and, as a loyal union man, he slugged scabs in the teamsters' strike of 1905; but Farrell recalls that his soft eyes suggested kindness and understanding.

To his son, James Francis Farrell has become a symbol of the striving and sorrows of working people. "Like my father," Farrell wrote to Saul Alinsky on January 24, 1942, "they go forth to the factories, the docks, the railroads, the wagons, the stockyards . . . and the work they do forms the basis of our entire civilization. I think of my father, of his fierce love of his family, his determination to keep his head high: there are thousands, millions and millions of men like him. They live on the streets I tramped as a boy in Chicago, and they live on similar streets in cities spread across this earth." Farrell has talked with such people in the subways of Paris, the pubs of London, and the slums of Dublin.

Mary Daly Farrell is supposed to have had, in all, fifteen children. Farrell is the second oldest of the six who lived to maturity: besides himself, William Earl, Helen, Joseph, John, and Mary. His birthplace, Farrell thinks, was 269 West Twenty-second Street on the near Southwest side of Chicago, slightly west of Wentworth and not many blocks from the Loop. Over the years the Farrell family, like the Dalys and many others, moved southward away from the downtown district. Some of Farrell's earliest memories of the city go back to his parents' home near Twenty-fifth Street and La Salle: he recalls the saloon on the corner, the black-shawled women, the Fuller Park Library where he withdrew some of the first books he read, the Rock Island tracks a half block away serving as the boundary of the Black Belt, and the small wooden houses, many on stilts, with no plumbing and lit by kerosene lamps.

Although James Francis Farrell was a strong, enterprising man, his wages as a teamster did not go far with children coming regularly. In 1907, when a new baby was about to arrive, Farrell was taken to live with his grandparents, the Dalys, who later also took in his sister Helen. The grandparents shared a comfortable apartment in retirement with three of their children. Farrell's Uncle Tom, a successful shoe salesman, and his Aunt Ella, a cashier who worked in the Loop at Allegretti's and later at several hotels, supported the household, which included the Dalys' youngest child, Farrell's Aunt Elizabeth (Bessie), whom he remembers as a beautiful auburn-haired young woman. The grandmother lovingly took in the three-year-old James, who bore the name of one of her dead children.

Farrell's removal at three to the Daly home, then in the 4900 block on Indiana Avenue, was the most important event of his childhood; for it had far-reaching personal and artistic consequences. He found himself in a well-to-do apartment house neighborhood of rising real-estate values. This world of brick and stone buildings with modern plumbing and central heating was in strong contrast to the poor neighborhoods his parents were to live in for many years. He remembers clearly, for instance, the cold, wooden cottage at 45th Place and Wells where his brothers and sisters caught diphtheria in 1918, and where one of them, his young brother Francis, died in his mother's arms for want of medical attention at the very time James was comparatively pampered.

Reflecting on the special circumstances of his childhood in a letter of March 21, 1946, to H. L. Mencken, Farrell wrote that the separation from his parents cut him off from the kind of family life normal for most boys and helped to give him a dual focus on personal relationships. In his fiction, he explained,

there is (I hope) something of an account or description of types of characters and types of action and conduct that is normal to the *milieu* I have described, and with this, something of an attempted revelation . . . from the inside; on the other hand, there is a certain attempted objectivity in presentation, and as I recall my moods and feelings when I wrote much of [my] fiction, I would feel so often outside of the material, and looking on. . . . There are many recollections I have of having felt different from others, and outside, outside of what was socially normal for them. Perhaps this is a complicated way, however, of saying that maybe I was a bit of a misfit.

Living with the Dalys had advantages, but at the cost of childish bewilderment and self-division. It plunged him into their family quarrels and led to tensions with his parents. It gave him the feeling of death at an early age: John Daly died in December, 1910, and Aunt Bessie, whom the small boy adored, soon after. Farrell's narrative method and the story he tells are anchored in his need to confront and identify himself amid the mysteries of his unusual childhood.

He entered the first grade of Corpus Christi Parochial Grammar School at Forty-ninth Street off Grand Boulevard in September, 1911; and he took his First Holy Communion in the spring of 1912. A rather lonely and intense boy, he was filled with dreams and was good at inventing games to play by himself. Having seen Ed Walsh's "no-hitter" that August, he was already a baseball fan when he started school. Sometimes he was called Young Ping after the White Sox player Ping Bodie, one of his idols. But, after 1913, when he was fitted with glasses, the nickname Four Eyes often made him miserable.

On May 1, 1915, having completed most of his fourth grade at Corpus Christi, he and his grandmother, his Uncle Tom, and his aunt Ella moved a few blocks south into the neighborhood made famous in *Studs Lonigan*. There his Uncle Bill joined them after the death of his wife in 1916; and in 1918 his parents, enjoying better times because of his father's promotion, took an apartment a few blocks away. Meanwhile, on May 1, 1917, the Dalys had rented the nearby second-floor apartment at 5816 South Park Avenue, overlooking Washington Park, where Farrell was to live for many years. Some of the boy's earliest glimpses of America outside Chicago came in 1919 and 1920 during vacations in Michigan with his Uncle Tom.

In the new neighborhood he attended St. Anselm's Parochial Grammar School, adjoining St. Anselm's Church, whose pastor was Father Gilmartin. Serious and still sensitive to the family division—and, at times, to the family turmoil—that made him different from other boys, he eagerly sought reassurance through companionship. He came to know many boys and girls in his immediate neighborhood and beyond, including a wide circle of friends who went to the nearby Carter Public School. His romantic dreams centered equally on baseball and girls, but he was better on the playing fields of Washington Park than at parties. By 1918 he was second baseman and lead-off man for the Hirsches, a local uniformed team; and he had also won a reputation for wrestling and boxing. For years his skill at sports gave him status in his boy's world. It was an avenue leading into the lives of others.

Of all his teachers at St. Anselm's, Sister Magdalen of the eighth grade influenced him most. Her perception of the loyalty and the "germ of destruction"—to use her phrase—in his character helped him toward self-understanding. Her kindness and her confidence in his ability dispelled his fear of punishment and made him want to excel in his studies. For the first time, his class in Christian doctrine became meaningful. Many years later he wrote in the manuscript "Sister" that, under her teaching, "religion became happier, not the dark and gloomy thing it had been. Instead of the faith being something that made me so afraid, it was something that I wanted to work for." He worked hard on his themes for Sister Magdalen, and he believed he would become a priest.

II   *High School and Night School*

Instead of attending a seminary, Farrell in 1919 entered St. Cyril High School (rebuilt in 1924 and renamed Mount Carmel), two miles southeast of his home. Uncle Tom paid his tuition. Founded in 1900 by the Carmelite Fathers, the school enrolled about two hundred and fifty boys from a wide area of the South Side. It offered two main curricula: a two-year commercial course and a four-year Classical course, which Farrell took and which is described in the 1920-21 catalogue as a study of "the Ancient Classics and History together with a foundation knowledge of Mathematics and Science so to refine and clarify and strengthen the mind of the student. . . ."

In an unpublished essay of 1929-30 concerning his youthful "mis-education," Farrell described his course of study as "a weak programme on the classical, Matthew Arnold plan, with the added element of religion, and a formal bow to physical science in the shape of a year of physics, and one of chemistry, five months of physiology, and a similar period to physical geography." He called the teaching authoritarian and routine. He remembered learning "that Socialists were monsters," that evolution "meant that men came from monkeys," and "that atheists could not really disbelieve in God." His high-school education, he wrote, completed the "process of devitalization which was started in the parochial schools. Scarcely one boy left St. Cyril to go out and approach life with a humane, tolerant outlook."[1] Thirty years later Farrell, who had partially changed his mind, felt that his high-school training had instilled basic moral values in his character.[2] The record shows that during his first two years he took either first honors (over 90) or second honors (85-90) in English, elocution, history, Latin, French, algebra, and Christian doctrine. Later, his grades declined, probably because he was disturbed by his father's illness and by his own uncertain direction in life.

Farrell was no rebel in high school. Gregarious and unquenchable in spirit, he was widely known and was active in the high-school fraternity Alpha Eta Beta. His letters of the period show him deeply involved in typical adolescent social intrigue. He thought and acted very much like his friends; and, above all else, he wanted the acceptance he did not fully receive. The girls he dated and his classmates sensed an indefinable and alien "difference" in him—the more remarkable, in retrospect, because of his athletic ability. "Jumps" Farrell won seven major letters in football, basketball, and baseball at St. Cyril; and for three years he was athletic editor of the monthly St. Cyril *Oriflamme.*

In that magazine his name often appears in the humor columns as a wit and a butt of jokes ("Farrell: 'Father, they pick on me all day.' Fr. Leo: 'Pretty poor pickins, I'd say.'").[3] There too several of his compositions were printed, including the first story about Danny O'Neil [sic] and one imitating Ring Lardner and H. C. Witwer. In his essay "My Beginnings as a Writer" Farrell describes some of his high-school writings and recognizes the influence of his teachers, in particular the studious and understanding Father Leo J. Walter, O.C.C., and the ambitious, authoritarian Father Albert Dolan, O.C.C. In those early years, he concludes, he wrote out of passion and interest, answering freely to a need for recognition and self-expression.

For two summers while he was in high school, Farrell worked as a telephone clerk in the Wagon Call Department of the Amalgamated Express Company offices on South Federal Street. After his graduation in 1923 he went back to his job, working up from $105 to $130 a month during his twenty-one months there. His wages were important to his grandmother and to his mother's family because of the decline in his uncle's business and because of his father's death. Feeling trapped and faced with a dreary future of office routine, he enrolled for night classes as a pre-law student at De Paul University in September, 1924. There he studied political economy, economic history, sociology, English history, and composition—and first read in Theodore Dreiser. "Sitting in the classroom on Randolph Street, with the night dark through the windows; tired, hearing the noise of nervous motor horns on Michigan Boulevard, recalling a nerve-racking day of work in the express office, knowing that lads and their girls were passing on Randolph Street below to see shows, to dance, to enjoy themselves and kiss and pet on dates, I felt as though I were like the man who had written *Hey-Rub-A-Dub-Dub.*"[4]

When the strain became too great, Farrell gave up his schooling and his job in March, 1925, and went to work as a gas-station attendant for the Sinclair Oil and Refining Company; but he saved money in order to enter the University of Chicago that June.

III *College Years and Literary Beginnings*

Farrell's college years (1925-29), during which he completed eight quarters, were crucial in his life because they gave him his profession. The University of Chicago opened his eyes to the world around him and to his past. It provided fresh ideas and a new faith, and it awakened his desire to be a writer. In short, the university gave him what he needed: understanding, purpose, direction. It offered a kind of earthly redemption, teaching him something of self-sufficiency and human potentiality. Farrell's return to his college experience in two novels, *My Days of Anger* (1943) and *The Silence of History* (1963), suggests its vital importance to him.

He came to college with a boundless but ill-defined ambition, with an organic ache for knowledge after years of intellectual starvation. Supporting himself by working as a filling-station attendant, he concentrated intensely upon his studies, at first upon the social sciences in particular. He read for hours in the library. Thus began a development as unpredictably intense, if not as inward, as Melville's unfolding eighty years before. Farrell's earlier reading had been more casual and restricted, although it had included Twain's *Huckleberry Finn* and *Tom Sawyer*, George Eliot's *Silas Marner*, Carlyle's *Sartor Resartus*, Conrad's *Lord Jim*, Ring Lardner's *You Know Me, Al*, and some Shakespeare. But, before he left the campus, Farrell, like Melville, had swum through libraries. William James, Dewey, George H. Mead, Nietzsche, Max Stirner, Bertrand Russell, Thorstein Veblen, R. H. Tawney, Sigmund Freud, Walter Pater, Ibsen, Chekhov, H. L. Mencken, Theodore Dreiser, Sherwood Anderson, Carl Sandburg, Sinclair Lewis, Ernest Hemingway, and James Joyce are some who were important to him. This intense application was reflected in a superior grade average of approximately 3.3 on a 4.0 scale.

After taking a composition course from Professor James Weber Linn, Farrell decided in the spring of 1927 to become a writer of fiction. He quit his job in July and dropped out of the university, telling himself he would succeed in his purpose or end in the gutter. That same month he hitchhiked to New York City with his friend Paul Caron and there earned his living as a salesman while he continued to write. *Bernard Clare* reflects that period of his life and his then rebellious spirit. He returned to Chicago in January; and, when he re-entered the university in March, he began to write aggressively critical articles for the student publications. Also he published book reviews in Chicago and New York newspapers. He continued to write thousands of words for Professor Linn and first placed one of his stories in a little magazine (*Blues*) in mid-1929. Jimmy the Genius, as a friend dubbed him, had made a beginning.

Farrell's college years taught him the value of hard work and self-discipline. They trained him in controversy and dissent, and they hardened him to hostility and enabled him to slug back effectively. More fundamentally, the university demonstrated the power of the mind, the role of ideas, in shaping his and every man's career and in helping men win a better life. Farrell's formidable ego, liberated by college from the authority of church and family, became free to expand. The once ardent Catholic had turned into a philosophic Naturalist and a pragmatist who aggressively affirmed the power of rational, liberal thought to improve society and who understood the role of literature in that effort. From his new vantage point, he was able to see and judge his past—the world of Danny O'Neill, Eddie Ryan, and Studs Lonigan; and he was beginning to translate that past into fiction.

As early as September, 1929, Farrell began work on his *Studs Lonigan* manuscript and related stories. Soon he published articles in *Plain Talk, The New Freeman,* and *Earth,* and tales in *Blues, Tambour,* and *This Quarter*—a small part of the extraordinary amount that he wrote at this time.

IV   *Paris*

In 1928, Farrell had met Dorothy Butler, a University of Chicago student. They were secretly married in the early spring of 1931 and left separately for New York City. For two days Farrell tried vainly to interest New York publishers in his manuscript on Studs; then he and Dorothy sailed on April 15 on the H.M.S. *Pennland* for France. The Farrells began their year in Paris with letters of introduction from Slater Brown, a list of hotels from Malcolm Cowley, and about eighty dollars in cash.

Farrell hoped that residence abroad would help him to get his novel or a volume of tales published. In 1930, Samuel Putnam, then associate editor of *This Quarter* in Paris, had given Farrell strong encouragement and had backed it up by persuading Edward Titus, the editor, to publish the story "Studs." After founding *The New Review*, Putnam wrote Farrell early in 1931 that he would like to publish a series of booklets starting with Farrell's writing.[5] Moreover, by early 1931 Farrell's alienation from his Chicago past was at a peak. As he wrote years later in the manuscript "Thoughts on Chicago and Paris," "My own differences were symbolized by books" because they "were doorways to a larger world. And that larger world had come to mean Paris."

But the year abroad proved to be a trying one both financially and emotionally. Farrell earned less than sixty dollars from short stories and six hundred dollars in advance payment from James Henle of the Vanguard Press for *Young Lonigan* and *Gas-House McGinty*. The Farrells had to borrow from Dorothy's mother and a few loyal friends, among them Martin J. Freeman. Even so, they fell four months behind in their rent; and, during the winter of 1932, Farrell was without decent shoes. Once he had to choose whether to buy soap or bread with his last franc. Julia Daly's death on October 2, 1931, affected him deeply; and late in the year Dorothy's baby, a boy named Sean, died five days after his difficult birth. For weeks, the world seemed dark and hopeless to Farrell. In his manuscript "Thoughts on Returning to Paris" he has written: "It was there that my youth really ended."

Nevertheless, the Paris year was productive and a turning point in his career. He quickly found that Montparnasse did not suit him. He had, as he states in a letter to James Henle, March 13, 1932, little sympathy with the "*transition* maniacs"; and he withdrew from the expatriates, who, he believed, had run away to damn America from Parisian cafés. There "everyone talks and little is said," he wrote to Walt Carmon on May 27, 1931. That same month the Farrells moved to the tranquil suburb Sceaux-Robinson, where they lived until the expected arrival of their child brought them back to the city in October. While in Sceaux, Farrell revised *Young Lonigan;* he completed many short stories, and, in a burst of energy generated by poverty, wrote most of *Gas-House McGinty* in about ten days.

During this period Farrell was buoyed up by Ezra Pound's belief in his work.[6] The two met in May, 1931, and Pound tried unsuccessfully to get Desmond Harmsworth in England to publish four of Farrell's stories as a book. Pound believed that Farrell's stories showed the arrival of a new writer, and in 1933 he wrote in an undated letter: "Am now waitin fer you to tackle the more developed protoplasm/ a novel that can hold both what you use in writing crit/ of philos/ and yr/ tough guys" (Farrell had shown Pound an article on the philosopher George H. Mead). Farrell liked Pound's advice that a collection of tales should center on one problem. For months he planned a book, called *Chamber of Horrors*, on the sexual problems of young Americans. As his idea of the work broadened, he changed the title to *These Chicagoans* which, in conception, was not unlike his first collection of tales, *Calico Shoes and Other Stories* (1934). Before he left Paris his stories had appeared in *The Midland, Readies for Bob Brown's Machine, The New Review*, and *Story; others* submitted to *Contempo, Pagany, The American Mercury,* and Peter Neagoe's anthology *Americans Abroad* were soon to appear; and, he had arranged for the French translation of *Young Lonigan* (1934). He also found time to read in Marcel Proust, William Faulkner, Thomas Wolfe, James Joyce, D. H. Lawrence, Henry James, Upton Sinclair, Leon Trotsky, Benedict Spinoza, Kathleen Coyle, and Djuna Barnes, among others.

V *New York City and Later Life*

When the Farrells disembarked at Hoboken in April, 1932, they had about fifteen dollars and had come to an America deep in economic trouble. But, as he wrote on April 22, 1947, to Meyer Schapiro, the Depression was not personally upsetting to him: "My uncle had been going down for years; the Farrells always were poor, I was poor, and very poor in Paris." A similar immunity to the fear of poverty, coupled with his seriousness of purpose, frequently has sustained him in the profession, as it did in 1935 when he turned down a tempting offer of $250 a week from Metro-Goldwyn-Mayer Studios so that he might continue writing *A World I Never Made*. Fortunately, soon after landing, Farrell learned that H. L. Mencken had purchased "Helen, I

Love You" for the *American Mercury.* Within a few days *Young Lonigan* was published and was being reviewed. James Henle staked Farrell to $150 for editorial work on parts of Lloyd Stern's *Star's Road.* In one way or another, the Farrells managed to survive economically.

From 1933 to 1935, Farrell lived for several periods at Yaddo, the rent-free writer's colony in Saratoga Springs, a privilege that measurably swelled the flood of his writing during the 1930's. For a number of years, beginning early in 1934, he contributed fairly regularly to the *Partisan Review;* and he became drama critic for the *Partisan Review and Anvil* in 1936. The following year he began a column in the *Socialist Call.* In addition to publishing *Gas-House McGinty* (1933), *Studs Lonigan* (1935), *A Note on Literary Criticism* (1936), and the first two Danny O'Neill novels, he placed many articles and stories, published three volumes of tales, and wrote the novelette *Tommy Gallagher's Crusade* (1939) during the 1930's, the decade of his greatest impact. A Guggenheim Fellowship for 1936-37 and, in January, 1937, a Book of the Month Club Award for *Studs Lonigan* (granted that year specifically for meritorious work that had not sold widely) recognized his accomplishment. The following month Farrell and the Vanguard Press were successful in their defense of *A World I Never Made* against the charge of indecency made in the important censorship case brought by John S. Sumner and the New York Society for the Suppression of Vice.

Upon Farrell's return from Paris, he had plunged directly into New York City's literary and intellectual life. The evening of his arrival he had met Horace Gregory and Edward Dahlberg, and in following months his friends and acquaintances multiplied at an astonishing rate. Some of them were Kenneth Burke, Josephine Herbst, Archibald MacLeish, Daniel Fuchs, Nathanael West, Granville Hicks, James Daly, Evelyn Scott, Henry B. Parks, Ferner Nuhn, Nathan Asch, Joseph Freeman, Carolyn Slade, and Kyle Crichton. He began his practice of helping launch other beginning writers: Edwin Rolfe, Sol Funaroff, Kenneth Fearing, John Cheever, and Nelson Algren are names near the top of a long, still growing list. He himself quickly became known as one of the most promising younger writers, a brash and voluble Irishman of "proletarian" origins and radical tendency, who was well read in the American pragmatists and in Marxian theory.

Farrell's early works had many favorable notices (but few sales); among these were some from Communist literary critics who praised his Studs Lonigan novels—displayed prominently in the Workers' Bookshop—as powerful portrayals of the decay of capitalist society. His prominence as a writer was recognized when he was asked to read a paper on "The Short Story" at the widely promoted and Communist-dominated American Writers' Congress of The League of American Writers held in New York City from April 26 to 28 in 1935. His avid interest in the 1936 Moscow trials, which he denounced in a speech late that year, was climaxed the following year when he traveled to Mexico with John Dewey and others to observe the proceedings of the Commission of Inquiry for the American Committee for the Defense of Leon Trotsky. This inquiry brought face to face two men who profoundly influenced Farrell.

Farrell then, as now, was an aggressive Irish individualist who, as he acknowledged in a letter to Robert Morss Lovett, August 9, 1945, had already learned that, "when you get into a controversy, you have to slug, you have to go right through it to the end, you have to really mean it." As early as May 10, 1932, he wrote to his friend Martin J. Freeman that the Communist leaders "don't give me any inspiration, and most of them are brainless. The literary ones are hopeless." Farrell soon came to believe that Communist critics like Granville Hicks and Mike Gold stood for the subjection of literature to political expediency and for the subversion of disinterested literary criticism. Not unnaturally, Farrell took every opportunity to make his views known and to deflate the reputation of books that he felt were meretricious and that seemingly had been well received by the Communist press mainly for political reasons. Notably, he attacked in print Jack Conroy's *The Disinherited,* Clara Weatherwax's *Marching! Marching!,* Robert Briffault's *Europa,* Clifford Odets' *Paradise Lost,* and Granville Hicks's *The Great Tradition.* As a result of the attacks, the Marxist critics began to scold Farrell and to counterattack.

Farrell's response was *A Note on Literary Criticism* (1936), in which he affirmed that literature has an esthetic and a functional value: it "must be viewed both as a branch of the fine arts and as an instrument of social influence."[7] He then proceeded to attack Marxist critics Gold, Hicks, Edwin Seaver, Isidor Schnei-

der, Philip Rahv, and others for crudely identifying literary merit
with propaganda value and for ignoring persistent esthetic
values. Using abundant examples, Farrell ridiculed the senti-
mentalism and narrow economic determinism of these revolutionary critics. They sloganized, he charged. They praised writing
for being proletarian, hopeful, or collective, and they damned it
for being bourgeois, defeatist, or individualistic. Farrell quoted
Granville Hicks, who was capable of writing: "'There is no
bourgeois novel that, taken as a whole, satisfies me. . . . I feel
within myself a definite resistance . . . that makes a unified
esthetic experience impossible'" (79). Speaking as one influenced
by the esthetics of George H. Mead and John Dewey, Farrell
charged that the basic failure of Marxist critics was the inability
"to realize the existence of pluralism in literature as literature
and as part of the larger processes that go to make up society"
(209).

Farrell's slashing attack established him as a primary target
for years to come for Communist reprisals. He was drawn in a
Gropper cartoon as one of the world's tiniest midgets; was called
Trotskyite, gangster of the pen, literary renegade; and was compared to an emotionally warped Ku Kluxer. Not unpredictably,
his books suffered at the hands of Communist or fellow traveler
reviewers. Farrell has the lasting distinction of having been an
early and a most effective spokesman against doctrinaire Marxian
criticism. If he sometimes slugged hard at opponents who today
seem trivial or weak, the reason is understandable; and the result
was to help re-establish sanity and integrity in criticism.

During the 1930's, Farrell lived through the final years of the
experience he has used systematically and at length in the major
cycles of his fiction—the action of *Yet Other Waters*, the final
volume of the Bernard Carr trilogy, ends in the fall of 1936—and
this account of his life does not attempt, therefore, to give his
later years in any detail. Since 1932 he has made New York City
his home, although for many years he has traveled widely in this
country and abroad as a lecturer. In addition, he has continued
to take an active part in the public life of his times. He has
generously given his efforts to organized labor, and he has also
been closely identified with such organizations as The American
Civil Liberties Union, The Workers' Defense League, PEN, The
American Committee for Cultural Freedom, and The Fund for

Intellectual Freedom. Politically, he has developed through various stages of anti-Stalinist socialism to the liberal internationalism of Adlai Stevenson, John F. Kennedy, Lyndon Johnson, and Hubert Humphrey; and for decades he has joined in political campaigns either as journalist or speaker. A consistent motive for much of his activity is his belief in individual and artistic freedom from shoddy cultural ideals, commercialism, censorship, political dictation, and dogmatic theory—a belief reflecting meanings implicit in his fiction.

To his fiction, at which he works each day wherever he is, he has given his greatest energy, his real life. Economically, this devotion has not been easy; and personal troubles have compounded his problems. In 1935, he and Dorothy Farrell separated. His later marriage to Hortense Alden, which also ended in divorce, was followed in 1955 by remarriage to his first wife and a second separation from her. He completed the original plan for his lifework more than a decade ago, yet with the energy of a man younger than his sixty-six years he continues to write his new cycle of fiction, A Universe of Time.

VI Journalist, Critic, and Essayist

During his long career Farrell has published hundreds of news reports, newspaper columns, letters to the editor, book and drama reviews, polemical pieces, articles, commentaries, and critical and personal essays. More unrelentingly than any of his novelist-contemporaries he has besieged the public with his views, and he has views on many subjects. Such writing "on the side" has helped him pay expenses, for his fiction has never earned large sums of money. But a more basic reason for his outpouring of journalism and criticism is his abiding interest and participation in the life around him—one of his syndicated columns was called "The World Around Me." Although this side of Farrell's career deserves extended consideration, the limits of this book permit only a brief commentary.

Farrell's earliest journalism appeared in Oriflamme, the high-school publication he served as sports editor. In college he used the columns of the Daily Maroon and other campus publications to attack university policies and practices that he disliked. He was soon writing reviews of novels and of nonfiction for Chicago and New York newspapers, contributing everything from simple booknotes to reflective, well-prepared commentaries. During the Depression years of the 1930's, his reviews brought in badly needed cash; and by 1938 he had placed over one hundred and sixty reviews in the New York *Sun*, the *New Republic*, *Scribner's*, the *New Masses*, and other outlets. Since then he has continued, on occasion, to write book reviews that are usually forthright and discriminating statements that focus honestly on the work.

During a financially difficult two-year period (1956-58) Farrell wrote literally thousands of unsigned, incisive editorials syndicated by the Alburn Bureau of Minneapolis in newspapers all over the country. The range of his topics is suggested by a few titles: "Propaganda Film," "India Needs Our Aid," "Baseball Is Changing," "Nasser on the Move," "Who Teaches Teachers?," "Kremlin Motives," "The John Dewey Myth," "The Control of TV." For many years he has been a semiregular contributor, in the role of commentator at large, to the Delhi magazine *Thought*. "The World Is Today," the most recent of his several magazine and newspaper columns, began in 1963 and appears in the Manhattan weekly *Park East*.

Farrell's skill not only as a journalist but as a sportswriter is evident in *My Baseball Diary* (1957), a lively book bringing together much of his best baseball writing. For any dedicated fan—especially any White Sox fan—it is a delightful mixture of baseball reminiscences, a few chapters from Farrell's Danny O'Neill novels, interviews with stars like Ray Schalk and Red Faber, profiles of other stars, and discussions of intriguing subjects such as the Black Sox, scouting, "them bums" the Brooklyn Dodgers (with whom Farrell toured), and the inalienable rights of fans—all by a lifelong fan himself.

It Has Come to Pass (1958) is, however, Farrell's journalism at its impressive best. The book is a wise, vivid account of Farrell's visit to Israel during the summer of 1956 when he traveled throughout the country and also into the camps for Palestinian Arab refugees. He talked with the people everywhere, especially the Jewish refugees from Arab lands and the Oriental immigrants. His reports leave a strong impression of the people's feelings and desires, the dynamism of the country, and the difficulties of integration. Farrell's knowledge of the problems that his own people faced as immigrants helped him to grasp the complexity of the problems facing the Israelis, and he wrote of them with insight and compassion. Moreover, his account is alive with a sympathetic understanding of Israel as a free and democratic society carrying forward much that is valuable in the Western tradition.

Of his collected essays, *The League of Frightened Philistines and Other Papers* (1945), *Literature and Morality* (1947), and *Reflections at Fifty and Other Essays* (1954) bring together some half a hundred of Farrell's short pieces. A few of these, such as the excellent "Dewey in Mexico," record profound personal experiences; others explore ideas in the fields of philosophy and history; many more are on literary topics. These include illuminating accounts of his own fiction (for instance, "How *The Face of Time* Was Written") and of the writings of Dostoevsky, Mark Twain, Chekhov, Theodore Dreiser, and Ernest Hemingway. Other literary essays characterize the proletarian short story in the 1930's, define the concept of Naturalism in fiction, and trace social themes in American Realist fiction of this century. Still others discuss the relationship of literature to political ideologies and moral codes. In these essays Farrell argued tellingly for the complete freedom of the artist from ideological constraint so that literature might remain "one of the most powerful means contrived by the human spirit for examining life."[8]

All through these essays Farrell's thinking about literature and the creative writer derives quite simply from what literature has meant to him. An unforgettable lesson of his life was that literature intensifies awareness. Because literature dramatizes human destinies and expands the "sense of the other" (*RAF*, 21), it liberates the personality and stimulates growth. Also it "humanizes the world" (*RAF*, 18) by assuring the cultural continuity that crowns life with meaning. Finally, as Farrell asserts in a letter to Frederick L. Allen, January 8, 1942, literature strengthens men's "spiritual resources" in a "precise way—it unfolds relationships, makes impressions, judgments, perceptions more sharp, opens up the mysteries of the world, the mysteries of human and social relationships, and the mysteries of the appreciations of forms, movements, and sounds."

As for the writer, his task is to give literary form to the life he knows. He conveys his vision through the quality of his characterizations and the structure he gives to events. The critic's role is to illuminate the creative work by exploring its internal re-

lationships and patterns and then to relate these to social processes. Farrell's own criticism of James Joyce and Tolstoi, for
instance, takes this approach, in keeping with his idea of the
two uses of literature, esthetic and functional, elaborated in
A Note on Literary Criticism.

Farrell's belief in the importance and autonomy of literature
lies behind his long, distinguished opposition to the literary
censor. Also it helps explain why many of his collected pieces
are essays in social criticism. He wants the serious American
writer to be able to work effectively, free from social repression
or manipulation, in a congenial cultural climate. Whether his
social criticism temporarily focuses on the literary cops of the
official left in the 1930's or on the genteel "Philistines" among
literary critics, it constantly employs touchstones of human freedom and of growth toward excellence. It identifies shoddy cultural products of the profit system ("The Fate of Writing in
America"), of Hollywood commercialism ("The Language of
Hollywood"), and of intolerant political doctrine ("The Literary
Popular Front Before the War"). It condemns what he believes
is intellectually regressive ("The Faith of Lewis Mumford") or
morally insensitive ("Moral Censorship and the Ten Command-
ments").

Clearly, Farrell's critical writings are of a piece with his fiction.
His social criticism, which attacks sources of cultural stagnancy
and human frustration, articulates much that his fiction dramatizes. His literary criticism, practical and theoretical, continually
returns to the idea of literature's liberating and energizing role
in society. Because Farrell knows that human effort and will can
lead to creative accomplishment, he also knows that among
man's deadliest enemies are those social forms that constrict the
mind and hamper the spirit. Such ideas animate nearly all of
his writing, whether critical or creative; for nearly all of it has
reference to the culture that educates men for good or ill.

If James T. Farrell is sometimes brash and pugnacious in his
social criticism, Jonathan Titulescu Fogarty, Farrell's comic character, his alter ego and latter day Mr. Dooley, is usually bland
and ingratiating, all sweetness and light. Fogarty's views are
best exposed in *The Name Is Fogarty* (1950) in which, as President of the Society for the Discovery of the World Brain, his
mission is to spread "seeds of happiness"[9] and to cultivate "smil-

ing souls" (46). In a speech dripping with the clichés of "free enterprise" and "individual initiative," Fogarty explains why Mr. Stalin's "Managerial Democracy" (21) with its Happiness Camps and YMCA clubs (GPU in Russian) was designed to promote universal happiness. Aided by his brother-in-law Abraham Lefkowitz O'Halloran, Fogarty stands ready to bring happiness to Americans after his own formula.

Fogarty's origins go back to 1933 in letters that Fogarty sent to Jack Kunitz. "At the time," Farrell has written in a letter to me of January 11, 1957, "the boys on the *New Masses* used to give me advice which I rejected, about participating in history instead of writing about it. Fogarty started to write letters about this" and about other things too. In 1934 he publicized the Legion of Indecency, a brotherhood of lechers whose required reading included the Studs Lonigan books. The next year he organized the Writers' Congress Left Opposition, a group whose manifesto called for "the development of three proletarian Prousts . . . within the period of three years" (Farrell to Kenneth Burke, April, 1935). A little later he formed a "Strike Committee of the Student Writers of the Granville Hicks School of Proletarian Writing and World Literature" (Farrell to Kenneth Burke, May, 1935) in order to "force justice into the class rooms."

Fogarty still writes an occasional piece. Unfortunately, the wit and satire of this bumbling old bore do not compare to his resourcefulness as an organizer.

VII *The Unity of Farrell's Fiction*

Before Farrell's fictional works are individually discussed, it is important to recognize the unity of his imaginative writing. With relatively few exceptions the subjects of his early books, like those on Studs Lonigan and Danny O'Neill, derived from the past he knew best: most frequently the family and social life that evoked deep emotional responses during his childhood and youth in Chicago. That crucial experience of his "plebeian" origins was in striking contrast to the rich intellectual heritage that he later found in books and that propelled him into his career. In his writing, early *and* late, he used the new perspectives and the expanded values embraced in college to portray truthfully his past experience with its core of personal development that continued long after he left Chicago. As he added tale to tale, it became increasingly clear that the intricately unified social world that he was objectively portraying cohered around an inner unity, which Farrell described in a letter to James Henle, May 14, 1951, as "the story of my own life, . . . of my own feelings, emotions, of my own unconscious, of myself in terms of development, integration."

This personal center, which unites Farrell's fiction at a deep level, supplies a drift of development, inner continuities of feeling. We can trace developing clusters of emotions in his characters, emotions Farrell also experienced: for instance, those associated with the need for love, acceptance, and status; romantic adoration; loneliness, rejection, and loss; rebellious and prideful self-assertion; nostalgia for the past. From such powerful and recurrent feelings flow patterns of action that are repeated with variations from book to book. These actions often have to do with family loyalties and estrangements and with the attempt to forge new social ties. They involve characters of many kinds and all ages who take various directions in life. But often they focus upon the son in an Irish-Catholic family and upon his efforts to discover his identity and win his desired place in life. Farrell's fiction constantly returns to the question of human destinies—how people became what they are, and where they are headed. As Farrell fills out his characters' lives, he explores growth, self-discovery, creativity—and frustration. These are his unifying themes.

Farrell has traced the destinies of scores of characters, but the major dramatic action in his work to date is the organic story of human emergence uniting the lives of Studs Lonigan, Danny O'Neill, and Bernard Carr. It is a story in which Studs represents the mean and ill-fated life that Danny rejects; Bernard, the creative life Danny chooses. "In a sense," Farrell wrote to Van Wyck Brooks on March 24, 1941, "the theme of all my fiction is the American way of life." The life Farrell knew and portrayed includes deprivation and crippling distortion of the personality but also the opportunity for growth and significant personal accomplishment. Because he paints a broad canvas of urban America, Farrell's subject ultimately becomes the unity of personal and national American development. As we shall see in Chapter 8, Farrell's poetry and his work in progress since 1958, *A Universe of Time,* do not violate the unified imagination that lies behind the body of his completed fiction.

CHAPTER 2

The Studs Lonigan *Trilogy—I*

I *Genesis and Composition*

Studs Lonigan: A Trilogy (1935) is composed of *Young Lonigan* (1932), *The Young Manhood of Studs Lonigan* (1934), and *Judgment Day* (1935). Usually considered Farrell's best work, the trilogy is a powerful, Realistic portrayal of the failure of understanding and potential growth in Studs, who dies an early, unheroic death. In June, 1929, Farrell began the long manuscript that became the first two volumes of the trilogy; and in New York's Brevoort Hotel on February 1, 1935, he finished the last revisions of *Judgment Day*. From the beginning, he wrote with the death of Studs in ·view; but most of *Judgment Day* was conceived after the first two novels were written.[1]

During the six years he worked on *Studs Lonigan,* he completed *Gas-House McGinty* (1933), a novel important to the writing of *The Young Manhood of Studs Lonigan* and *Judgment Day,* and scores of short stories.[2] Some of these were collected in *Calico Shoes* (1934) and in *Guillotine Party* (1935), and many continued the exploration of the Studs Lonigan neighborhood. Also during these years he began to write Danny O'Neill's story, the fictional account of his own early life: on February 5, 1934, he sent his editor James Henle the first draft of part of *A World I Never Made* (1936).

Actually, Farrell had wanted to write Danny's story before he conceived his plan for *Studs Lonigan.* But, as he explained in 1938, "I felt that I was unprepared, too inexperienced in both writing and in life, to begin it." A new consciousness of the craft of writing had convinced him "that the writer should submit himself to an objective discipline, that he should get outside of himself and seek to describe sections of the world which he knew. I decided that the writer should begin in such a manner rather than by licking his own wounds and lacerating his own adolescence on paper."[3] Reserved for later use, Danny remained alive in Farrell's mind as he concentrated on Studs.

The tale "Studs," written for Professor Linn in 1929, became the germ of the trilogy. By April, 1931, when he and Dorothy left for Paris, Farrell had completed a substantial portion of the first two volumes. Following his return to New York a year later as *Young Lonigan* was being published, he completed *The Young Manhood of Studs Lonigan* while living at Yaddo. He immediately began *Judgment Day,* the Depression novel that concludes the trilogy and passes judgment on the sinner Studs and on the family and society that fostered him.

II *Setting, Action, and Narrative Method*

The *Studs Lonigan* trilogy covers fifteen years—one-half of Studs's life—from June 16, 1916, the day of President Wilson's renomination and of Studs's graduation at fourteen from St. Patrick's Grammar School, to a day in August, 1931, when Studs, almost thirty, dies in bed. The scene is Chicago, and the action goes from World War I to the early days of the Depression; Studs declines from the strong young fighter with ambitions to be a war hero to the impoverished, dying weakling. For twelve of those years, roughly covered by the first two volumes, he lives near Fifty-eighth Street, first on Wabash Avenue and then on Michigan Avenue. The neighborhood is middle class and partly Irish Catholic.

The Studs Lonigan district proper is predominantly an apartment building area of thirty-six city blocks, six in each direction, directly west of Washington Park. It is bounded on the north by Fifty-fifth Street (Garfield Boulevard), on the south by Sixty-first Street, on the east by South Park Avenue, and on the west by State Street. The core of the district lies between Fifty-seventh and Fifty-eighth streets and Wabash and Calumet avenues. In these four blocks are the homes of many of the characters. On Fifty-eighth Street are the stores and restaurants they patronize, the Carter Public School and playground, Charley Bathcellar's Billiard Parlor and Barber Shop, and the local "L" station. Studs goes into nearby Washington Park a great deal; and he is occasionally seen outside his district, as when he joins the Armistice celebration in the Loop, or goes to Louisa Nolan's Dance Hall, or joins in the New Year's Eve party in the Black Belt. In the original neighborhood of the first two volumes, self and society are closely identified. Studs, who usually acts with his gang or in accord with its values, finds in his group an image of himself to respect.

In the spring of 1928 Studs's father sells his Michigan Avenue apartment building to a Negro buyer. The family moves several miles to the southeast to a new building near Seventy-first Street and Jeffrey Avenue, the setting for most of *Judgment Day*. This neighborhood is serviced by the South Shore line of the Illinois Central, and it is a few blocks from Lake Michigan to the east and Jackson Park to the north. Wealthier than the other area, it includes blocks of impressive private homes and well-kept apartment buildings. Also it is well away from the steady push of Negro population that drove the Lonigans from their apartment building on Michigan Avenue. It is not dominated by the Irish Catholic community.

Ironically, here Studs's fortunes rapidly decline; his fate closes in on him not long after he has left his earlier, more smothering neighborhood. In *Judgment Day*, the old gang is dispersed, Studs is engaged to be married, and he moves around more freely and broadens his interests. The view of Chicago enlarges; and, for the first time, we see Studs briefly outside the greater Chicago area as he returns from Terre Haute. There is a marked increase in various social and economic concerns as Depression times drive Studs into a corner and bring new realizations. Studs now thinks about his declining stocks almost as much as his weakening body. In *Judgment Day*, transplanted from his earlier environment, Studs flowers in a deformed, dwarf-like way. Despite the belated Indian-summer growth, he is seen as all the more lost and alone, in keeping with his actual puniness and isolation.

Farrell uses the urban setting in *Studs Lonigan* primarily to illuminate character, and he includes very few extended descriptions of the milieu. Somewhat like James Joyce in *Ulysses*, Farrell assumes an acquaintance by the reader with the setting. Farrell's Realism which is more phonographic than photographic, relies heavily upon dialogue to give a sense of character and to carry the narrative forward. Farrell's picture of Chicago has little visual vividness; unlike Dreiser's, it minimizes visual documentation for its own sake. For Dreiser, who was impressed by Chicago's vigor and youth, the city's expansive, changing quality awakened a sense of adventure and evoked awe. That spirit and his desire to preserve the wonders of a shifting scene are reflected in his documentary descriptions.

But Farrell's Chicago is another matter. By 1916 Studs's—and Farrell's—neighborhood was relatively settled. It did not yet feel seriously threatened by the Negro population. Social patterns had congealed. Studs's parents and many of their neighbors are self-made, middle-class people not long out of the Old World. They cling to what they have with a frugal materialism. A sense of stale completion, not newness or dynamism, saturates Studs's neighborhood. Stereotyped thoughts, inflexible habits, and a potential for growth choked off at the roots, mark Studs and his friends. Since it is Studs's sense of life that the trilogy communicates, it is appropriate that documentation and description of setting are minimal, for these imply discriminating awareness or an emotional impulsion by the observer. Studs's discrimination is usually rudimentary, and he bottles up his emotions.

The physical environment is thus introduced sparingly and is incidental to Studs's movements, his inner preoccupations, or his needs of the moment. Usually the notation of place is brief, and it is almost invariably accurate. Making minor allowance for changes brought by time, we can still see in the very location specified in the book the exact apartment building, alley, or drugstore that filters through Studs's consciousness. Lucy's gray-brick house or Mr. Lonigan's apartment building may be readily found today. If Studs runs a stick along an iron picket fence in a certain block on Prairie or passes a yellow-brick convent flanking the St. Patrick School playground on the north, likely enough that fence and convent still stand. Descriptions given in such a manner gain in naturalness and inevitability.

More important, the method anchors the characters to the environment. We know where a character is and in which direction he is moving. Lonewolf Lonigan, toy gun in pocket, emerges from Washington Park at Cottage Grove Avenue, proceeds east down Fifty-third toward Ellis, turns south on Ellis, east on Fifty-fifth, and finally ends up "in back of a telephone post at Fifty-sixth Street in the alley between Kenwood and Kimbark."[4] This literalism has significance; for such passages suggest that the characters are tied tightly, though not inescapably, to a maze of ugly streets and buildings, a connection typifying their spiritual limitations. Moreover, through this method, different places, such as the corner of Fifty-eighth and Indiana and the "L" station near Fifty-eighth and Calumet, take on symbolic values and help dramatize conflicts in the story. Farrell's use of place also reinforces his irony, as the relationships of Studs and of Mickey Flannagan to the fireplug at Fifty-eighth and Prairie illustrate.

In his two neighborhoods Studs lives about 5,435 days beyond his graduation from eighth grade; the trilogy presents portions of his experience from sixty-five of those days: fifteen in *Young Lonigan*, thirty-one in *The Young Manhood of Studs Lonigan*, and nineteen in *Judgment Day*—an approximate count. The action is, therefore, selective and discontinuous. Time gaps between the episodes range from a few minutes to over three years. The episodes from Studs's life are usually precisely located in time and are chronologically arranged. His portrayed experience on a given day may be divided into several episodes or presented in a continuous action, and it may include more or less than a chapter. The development within an episode may be intensive and slow, particularly if Studs's consciousness is explored. At the other extreme, it may be extensive and quick moving—even jerky if the action is external and is presented discontinuously in brief vignettes, as in Chapter 6 of *The Young Manhood of Studs Lonigan*. Thus, fifteen years of Studs's life are opened up to the reader in selected segments of time, representative stretches of the stream of experience leading to his death.

The distribution of these years over the three volumes emphasizes the over-all structure, which follows the curve of Studs's life. *Young Lonigan* covers about five months in the second half of 1916, although nearly all the action falls within two months. *Judgment Day* covers six months from February to August, 1931. The first volume shows Studs choosing a way of life: he scorns learning, breaks with Lucy, joins the Prairie Avenue gang, and becomes "a man" at fifteen after being with Iris. The last volume shows the outcome of his choice: he is an insignificant laborer; loses his work, money, and health; gets his girl Catherine pregnant but does not truly love her; and dies a miserable death. In

Young Lonigan, life as he wills it seemingly opens up for Studs; in *Judgment Day,* it relentlessly closes in. Farrell rounds out the action to fit this pattern.

For example, in *Young Lonigan* Studs at fourteen thinks of his school as a jailhouse, and his first thought in the trilogy is: "Well, I'm kissin' the old dump goodbye tonight" (3). But, at the end, he comes to think of the world as a cage; and, without an education, he can find no place in it. During his first summer, Studs thinks of looking for a job: he feels he has plenty of time; but, at the end, time runs out as he looks desperately for work. In both volumes the focus is on Studs. Experience is mainly given in his idiom. Notable exceptions are the revelations of Paddy Lonigan's consciousness at each end of the fifteen-year span. These frame Studs's life, ironically illuminating its origins and its significance. Thus the first and third volumes give the crucial beginning and end of Studs's adulthood, his choice and its outcome, with relative concentration and unity.

The ironically titled middle volume, *The Young Manhood of Studs Lonigan,* spans twelve and one-half years, from April 6, 1917, to January 1, 1929. Studs tries to join the army, leaves school, begins work as a painter, and graduates from tough young "punk" to accredited street barbarian. We see him at home, in church, at work, and with his friends. He vacillates from dissipation to random attempts at reform; he changes from the strong fighter and crude idealist to the helpless, bloodied figure, to whom "most things are just plain crap" (189), who is draped around the fireplug at Fifty-eighth and Prairie. *The Young Manhood of Studs Lonigan* represents the middle period of his life, the bulk of his experience, the stages of corruption between initial choice and final consequence. Appropriately, the coverage is discontinuous but representative. The action is a series of penetrations into key moments of his experience. Although the focus remains on Studs, the interchapters place the drift and setting of his life in perspective; for we see Davey Cohen and Andy Le Gare in far-off cities and share the feelings of the older generation or of the idealistic Danny O'Neill.

Thus the trilogy conveys Studs's immediate sense of existence, not for a day but for fifteen years in two contrasting Chicago neighborhoods. The action is episodic, but the episodes are bound together by a narrative line that follows the curve of his life and traces his changing feelings toward it. This method creates a sense of time's flow, the unceasing succession of moments, days, weeks, and years in Studs's career. The reader is more fully aware than Studs of the significance of the flow, for Farrell has underscored time's passage by meaningful devices. Headlines, songs, and newsreels fix episodes in the time stream and relate Studs's life to the current of national life. Studs's young brother, Martin, grows in toughness as Studs declines; and the stages are carefully marked. The spaced death of Studs's friends and the falling quotations on Imbray stock in *Judgment Day* are measures of time's effects. Studs insistently questions "What time is it?" or "What shall we do now?" His boredom, his misuse of leisure seen in repeated incidents, reinforces the reader's sense of time's slow but ravaging passage in his life.

The use of time in *Studs Lonigan* supports Farrell's moralistic view of Studs's life as a darkening progress toward death, and Studs's attitudes toward time reinforce that view. At first, confident of success, he yearns for the future and glorifies his role in it. But, as Farrell has written, "this dream of himself turns backward. . . . More and more it becomes a nostalgia image turned toward the past."[5] Studs even sees Catherine, his fiancée, in the image of Lucy, long since lost. Future time becomes increasingly empty for him. Occasionally in later life, frustrated and weakened, he indulges dreams of future greatness, but he is usually aware of the widening gap between reality and the early dream. Characteristically, he comes to feel that every minute carries him away from his good "kid days . . . just as if he was on a moving express train which was shooting him forever away from some place where he very much wanted to be, and all the while carrying him nearer and nearer . . . to his own death" (5-6).

But Studs sees no hope in death. Catholic though he is, he has no living belief in heaven as a real possibility. His meager sense of blessedness is narrowly secular and personal. Often it is merely a reaction to the haunting fear of death. Even his boyhood dream of bliss with Lucy curls around thoughts of death. After he loses her, he dreams that Old Man Death chases him with a scythe and that he runs to her. At other moments, his thoughts of death make him resolve to be hard, healthy, tough. He would substitute the word "healthy" for "faithful" in the verse "Heart of Jesus, my true friend / Make me faithful to the end" (*YMSL*, 228). He pictures himself in old age as a patriarch who has outlived, outloved, and outfoxed his contemporaries—a solitary victor in life's competition.

Studs cannot conceive a communal heaven on earth, except as "shines" and "kikes" might be put in their place to make the world safe for white men. He has no sense of being part of a common dynamic movement toward a possible better existence here or in another world. Time becomes erosion to him. Thus the progress of time toward his death, reflected through his consciousness and traced at varying pace through discontinuous episodes within the time stream, creates a powerful double effect: the strong sense of time's shaping passage and the static heaviness of life standing still, a stagnant death-in-life quality.

Studs the Catholic has a lively sense of hell. Damnation is meaningful to him, as heaven never is, because his life is a hell to his secret, affectional self. In his confident moments he may think of death as blankness, as an unfortunate oblivion that will terminate his earthly success. But, more often, it is the doorway to eternal torment. His image of hell, like Father Gilhooley's, is a sea of fire and moaning people: "all the heads of the damned kept bobbing up, bobbing up. And everybody there was damned for eternity, damned to moan and burn, with only their heads now and then bobbing up out of the flames" (*YL*, 190).

This vision of existence is a metaphor of the content and method of the trilogy. For we see Studs and many of his friends repeatedly bobbing up, disappearing, bobbing up, in a kind of earthly damnation. His sense of life is therefore implicit in the method used to communicate his experience. This same method also conveys, obliquely and ironically, Farrell's view of existence. Naturalist Farrell, like Studs, believes that time brings no security, here or in another world; but the metaphysics and the ethical implications of Farrell's belief are at odds with Studs's dreary supernaturalism.

Farrell's method of presenting his characters discontinuously in segments of time, chronologically arranged, creates a tissue of ironic meanings. The reader who sees each person at different times amidst various circumstances, notices change: growth and success, failure and disintegration. He compares one person to another and observes shiftings, transpositions, reversals. He sees, too, that change seems hardly to affect some characters, who express virtually the same obsessions, the same clichés, from first to last. Throughout the trilogy, the reader sees Farrell's people against the backdrop of their changing past. He becomes aware of meanings reverberating backward and forward in the action as past and present become mutually illuminating and raise anticipations of the future. So the reader feels time doubly: as an invincible sweep of action toward a terminus and as segments of a broken continuum that make possible vivid, ironic juxtapositions dramatizing time's meaning in terms of character.

This effect may be felt even in minute details: Studs's and Father Shannon's sneers; Les Coady's constant complaints about his job; the gang's routine kidding of Barney Keefe about his false teeth; tough Studs atop the fireplug at Fifty-eighth and Prairie, and rolled by a Negro under it; parallels between Studs and Davey Cohen; reversals between Studs and Muggsy McCarthy, or Studs and Mickey Flannagan. As Farrell makes the data of human personality and fortune vividly meaningful through his handling of time, entire scenes emerge as units of comparison. For example, a key passage for understanding Studs occurs in *Young Lonigan* when, as a young "punk," he is introduced into Charlie Bathcellar's poolroom. The older guys let Studs in on a practical joke—filling moronic Nate's pipe with horse manure and pretending it is fine tobacco. Studs feels good because he is stamped as an equal; ironically, he attains brotherhood through a sadistic action. When he is taken into the poolroom, he is thrilled at the sight of the tables and at a group of the lads playing poker. He is elated as he washes his hands in the filthy washroom. A few minutes later he stands with the boys on the street, watching the neighborhood dopes go by—the unalive, conventional people of Fifty-eighth Street compared to whom the gang seems strong, young, and free. Here we see some of Studs's deepest feelings—his longing to count, to be alive. But we also see those feelings, basically admirable, becoming attached to corrupt objects, the idealism becoming distorted. This episode parallels the lyrical scene in which Studs and Lucy sit together in a tree. Here again Studs finds acceptance and fulfillment. Again he senses the soaring promise of life and feels part of something finer and bigger than himself. But only with the boys in the poolroom does he find a structure of practices that offers direction for his feelings, including those for girls. The flowing emotions aroused by Lucy prove unreliable guides for other parts of his experience. These two episodes dramatize a crucial early development in Studs and make clear the continuity of his ongoing self. As milestones in his destiny, they help to define the meaning of time in his life.

III   *The Personal Basis*

Neither Farrell's use of an objective narrative method nor his decision to put aside Danny O'Neill's story should blind us to the intensely personal nature of *Studs Lonigan*. The trilogy, rooted in Farrell's personal past, arose primarily from memories and not from notebooks kept for purposes of documentation. Especially the first two books draw upon deeply absorbed, early impressions, as Farrell indicates in an unpublished manuscript, "The Story of *Studs Lonigan*": "The perceptions, the impressions, much of the language all came to me as material of life at a time when I had not the slightest idea that I would ever compose such a work as this trilogy. The pattern of life, the types of conduct, the milieu of this work was not studied, observed, classified and catalogued by me with any idea that it would be used as literary material." Farrell's sociological interest in his neighborhood when he was a college student presumably is an exception to this claim.

On July 26, 1934, Farrell wrote to James Henle that *Judgment Day*, compared to the first two volumes, depended more on his invention and less on remembered characters and events. Memories absorbed long before the writing are less important in it than in the other books, and the time of the action, 1931, was reasonably fresh in mind as he wrote. Moreover, he wanted to give in this Depression novel a strong sense of Studs's world "constantly knocking at the door of his consciousness," as he explained to Henle on December 3. To this end, he used devices like newspaper headlines, and he developed representative scenes to underscore the social message. The result is a picture of Studs's environment more diversified and pronounced than that in the first two books, but one more obviously manipulated.

Also, showing the Realist's concern for accuracy, Farrell asked a number of friends to supply or verify some details for use in the novel. Despite these qualifications, *Judgment Day*, like the rest of the trilogy, is a profoundly personal statement.

For years, Farrell accepted many of the values that prevailed in his family and neighborhood. But, by 1929, the university had liberated him intellectually, and Dorothy Butler had taught him something of love. The parochial high-school athlete whom girls had rarely liked to date twice found in the late 1920's a world responsive to ideas and desire. Most of the barriers of his youth were dissolving, and *Studs Lonigan* was a result of the new-found liberation and a consolidation of it.

In the Introduction to *Studs Lonigan* Farrell wrote of his trilogy: "My attitude toward it and toward my character here is essentially a simple one. 'There but for the grace of God go I'" (xv). This statement is fundamentally true, but we may doubt that Farrell's attitude is quite so simple. To be sure, thankfulness, humility, pity, awe, and especially understanding are implicit in the writing: the many episodes of the trilogy lead to a fate Farrell had escaped. Moreover, in some repects the author's identification with Studs is close. The brooding fear of death, the lyrical picture of boyhood loves, loyalties, and games were Farrell's as well as Studs's.

But the trilogy also was written by a man not long converted to a life of imagination and reason. He was exorcising some of the evil potentialities that his past had held for him and that his future might still hold for him under the stress of possible failure. Farrell's indignant rebellion against his culture charges the writing with an emotional tension even though, through Danny, it is expressed in one notable scene only. Unquestionably, *Studs Lonigan* is in part indictment and aggression; but it is also triumph, for Farrell overcame the region and its cultural limitations. This triumph was earned by dogged work and sheer will power, and it yielded an awareness of values and truths Studs never grasped. So we return to awareness and understanding—key concepts in the complex attitude implicit in *Studs Lonigan*. It is no accident that in one way or another Farrell reverts to these values in his criticism and his fiction. In the final effect produced by *Studs Lonigan*, the need for illumination dominates lesser motives buried in the writing.

The epigraph to *Young Lonigan* quoted from Dewey's *Human Nature and Conduct* is to the point here. Dewey had written: "The poignancy of situations which evoke reflection lies in the fact that we do not know the meaning of the tendencies that are pressing for action." Dewey's abstraction expressed for Farrell what he was trying to do in writing about Studs: to understand and reveal through art the meaning of tendencies felt in his own life and observed in Studs's. The short story "Studs," from which the novel grew, sprang out of a situation that evoked reflection: the wake of Studs and the death-in-life he had lived and partially shared with Farrell. Studs's death symbolized to Farrell the final meaning of those tendencies pressing for action: the waste of failing to live with understanding and love even though these were within Studs's reach and not foreign to his basic character. *Studs Lonigan* is a story of meagerness and spiritual deprivation in the face of genuine possibilities of self-fulfillment through reason and love. It is a tragedy in the failure of understanding.

Some of the complex personal origins of *Studs Lonigan* are revealed in a letter written by Farrell to James Henle on January 15, 1946, a time of emotional turmoil immediately after the death of his mother. The letter touches on the inner motivation of the trilogy and on the creative explosiveness of Farrell's experience at Studs's wake in the spring of 1929. There Farrell met a number of old acquaintances who awoke vivid memories of his past, and his letter speaks in particular of two events that he remembered best at the wake. One was Red Kelly[6] scoffing at him upon learning he was a campus reporter. The other was Loretta Lonigan weeping for Studs— and Farrell's distinct impression that she could not really have loved Studs. Because Red Kelly, Loretta, and Studs had once been personally important to Farrell, they called up buried feelings.

Farrell's letter to Henle reveals that he and Red Kelly had been hostile from their first meeting in 1916. In the trilogy Kelly typifies, more purely than any other character except Weary Reilley, the ugly qualities of the Fifty-eighth Street gang. Significantly, it is Kelly, who, with Studs and Barney Keefe,

insults Danny as he is walking home with an armload of books
after having vowed to purge from his consciousness the dead
world of Fifty-eighth Street.

To Farrell, Loretta Lonigan typified a series of boyhood
sweethearts and the lofty feelings they inspired. She was the
best friend of Helen Scanlan, Farrell's first girl in the neighborhood; and, for a short time, Loretta stood first in his affections.
To his delight and guilt she once kissed him during a game
of tin-tin, her lips sweet with candy—the basis of the similar
scene between Studs and Lucy. Their little affair did not last
long, but her presence at the wake aroused memories of the
idealistic love for many girls that had moved him so strongly
in his youth.

Farrell's relationship with the real Studs was complex and
sensitive. Studs was one of the first two boys Farrell met when
he moved to the Fifty-eighth Street neighborhood, and he ad-
mired Studs as a boy might admire his older brother.[7] His
letter to Henle states: "I was always interested in him and
wanted his good will." After Farrell handily won a fist fight,
Studs and his friends took him as a mascot. Farrell basked in
Studs's praise of him as a fighter, for Studs was one of the best
scrappers for blocks around. Farrell remembers intensely wanting Studs to win his fights and wondering whether Studs could
whip Red Kelly. Also, as Farrell keenly realized, Studs came
from a middle-class family that was socially and economically
superior to the Farrells and the Dalys. Studs's father, a plaster-
ing contractor, owned an apartment building and drove a big
Packard.

In contrast to Studs's early acceptance of the younger boy,
Studs treated Farrell harshly in the later poolroom days. The sympathetic relationship changed to one between "tough guy" and
"goofy young punk." The old understanding appeared only
rarely; and, as Farrell continued his education, the breach
widened. When they met for the last time in November, 1928,
on Randolph Street in front of the Chicago Public Library, Studs
was accompanied by two friends. Farrell wrote to Henle: "I
talked with them, trying to impress them with casual cynicism,
and I was not dismayed, not apologetic for my difference.
Sensitive to Studs being there, I casually ignored him, and he
put out his hand and asked me if I didn't want to say hello

to him. This was a personal victory for me." Although Farrell
had come to despise Studs's ways, Studs still awakened mixed
feelings in him.[8]

The short story "Studs" reflects Farrell's ambivalent attitude.
He wrote that a dirty trick had been played on Studs when
he was given Extreme Unction and was sent to heaven, for
without poolrooms and brothels he would be miserable. The
criticism is directed at the Catholic Church and at Studs's habits.
He is labeled a slob who "would have grown into fatter and fatter decay" had he lived.[9]

He is the former adventurous boy who had "disappeared in
slobbish dissipation," his pleasures "compressed within a hex-
agonal of whores, movies, pool, alky, poker, and craps." He
had hung around the poolroom "waiting for something to hap-
pen." But in heaven his boredom would be even greater, for
he would be alone with the churchgoers, whose piety had not
helped him on earth. Farrell commented to Henle in his letter:
"I had rejected Heaven, then. My mother, and all of the good
people would go to Heaven." Slob that Studs became, he still
suggests Farrell's earlier feelings for the older boy. In his unenlightened way, Studs dissented from stuffy respectability.

In the short story Studs is not left unconscious in the gutter
nor shown nastily prurient in a burlesque house as he is in
the trilogy, although we see him briefly in a drunken rage. He
looks handsome in the coffin, and his face bears no trace of
suffering. Far away from dirty Fifty-eighth Street, his grave at
Mount Olivet "will be soaked and soppy, and fresh with the
wet, clean odors of watered earth and flowers." The unnamed
narrator, later to be christened Danny O'Neill, remembers events
of Studs's life that suggest a certain integrity.

In the trilogy Farrell develops his mixed vision. Still weak,
Studs is betrayed by ignorance. He embraces the platitudes
of middle-class Catholic morality, and he tries to make his
dreams come true by willingly adopting the widespread corruptions of his streetworld. Stereotyped habits overwhelm his
good impulses. His judgment day approaches painfully as he
lives on into that slobbish period of decay that he had partially
escaped in the short story by dying at twenty-six. Although
he gets his girl, she is second best; and their fumbling, unsatis-
factory love leads only to despair. Yet in *Judgment Day* his

decline marks a gain, for his predicament brings out qualities of consideration and tact. His tolerance of others grows, and his feeling for his parents and Catherine can be genuinely unselfish.

Studs becomes more realistic about himself: He sees the pretentiousness of his past opinion that he was the real stuff. He understands that he has lived on dreams, and he recognizes the trap he is in. "Swell Lonewolf now, he was, hemmed in on every side" (*JD*, 352). He recognizes his mistake in stopping school, and at times he seems to understand that his miserable predicament was caused not by the bad breaks of the game, a favorite immature philosophy of his, but by Studs Lonigan himself, "an all-around no-soap guy." "Every time a fly ball had been hit to him with men on the bases, he'd muffed it" (*JD*, 244). He comes to feel that "He must have the streak of a real bastard in his make-up" (*JD*, 333). Toward the end, he senses the horror in his relationship with Catherine, whom he sees as a stranger. Despairingly he recognizes his life-error: "Now there was no let-up. All day and always now he would have to keep himself going, and all the boozing and things he had done in his life, they had sure backfired on him. And he had never really been happy" (*JD*, 351-52). Farrell's emotional ties with the real Studs, who had admitted him into his friendship and then roughly excluded him, lead ultimately to the portrait of a man whose crippled humanity condemns himself, falteringly and darkly, for the self-destruction he has worked.

Although Danny O'Neill is the author's autobiographical character in the trilogy, Farrell identifies with Studs in many respects. There are the boy's imaginative play, his sensitivity to criticism, his preoccupation with sex and consequent bewilderment, and his conventional conscience. Both learn the feel of a clean tackle on the gridiron; both bear psychological scars often found on the sons and grandsons of immigrants; and neither becomes a large man physically, although Studs is the smaller. We also see the similarity in some deep-seated attitudes. Like Farrell, Studs has a strong sense of destiny and looks for the "something more" (*YMSL*, 159) just ahead, never quite seized. The idealistic strain in Studs is expressed in ways not far removed from Farrell's experience: Studs's early zeal for martyrdom in the fourth grade, his desire to lead and to win prominence, and his wish to right what seems wrong, as at the Christy initiation.

Studs's need for understanding and his accompanying sense of loneliness are important in this connection. His need is not met by his parents and is one reason he likes Helen Shires. His "old not-belonging feeling" (*YL*, 37) leads him to find comfort in daydreams. Later, he thinks of himself as a "lonely and unhappy adventurer" going through life "to some dangerous and unknown end" (*JD*, 16). These feelings and their causes have fairly close parallels from Farrell's early life. In *Studs Lonigan* the vein of insecurity, of failure, and of time and death as man's enemies are allied to Farrell's uncertainty about his personal future as well as to his Naturalistic philosophy. Moreover, in the face of mounting ill fortune, Studs's defiance of the world, his defensive "hard-guy" stance—chin up, ready to take whatever is dished out—is a debased form of a stoical attitude Farrell has expressed ever since his reading of Bertrand Russell's "A Free Man's Worship" in the 1920's.[10]

Clearly, much of the trilogy's force derives from the author's imaginative identification with his characters, an identification falling within a larger pattern of rejection that applies to Studs and his kind. Farrell's objectivity is infused with strong personal emotion. The genuineness of his fiction arises from deeply felt experience.

CHAPTER 3

The Studs Lonigan *Trilogy* — *II*

I *Self and Society*

When Farrell began to write *Studs Lonigan* in June, 1929, he was weighing the problem of individual character in relationship to environment. Fully aware of economic determinism in human life, he considered the possibility of making Studs a slum dweller. But he decided that a slum setting, with its emphasis on paralyzing material poverty, would obscure an important meaning in his novel: the effect of spiritual poverty upon character. He proceeded to use his own boyhood neighborhood, one that he described in a notebook of that time as "bourgeois" and "unhappy," as having "all the deadness that comfort loving middle-classness implies."[1]

Furthermore, he believed that individual character was cause as well as effect, for each person interacts dynamically with his culture. In 1940 he defined his early view, one that he still accepts: "I hold a functional conception of character, viewing it as a social product embodying the reciprocal play of local influences on the individual, and of the individual on society. I am concerned with the concrete processes whereby society, through the instrumentality of social institutions, forms and molds characters, giving to the individual the very content of his consciousness."[2] He adopted this view after his reading of John Dewey and George Herbert Mead in the 1920's, and he put it this way in the undated manuscript "The Story of *Studs Lonigan*": "Environment affected character, and character itself is a social product which is a result of society. In turn, character affects and changes environment." He added that Studs was not conceived as "an unwilling victim of environment."

There is little doubt that the trilogy shows character as being molded by social values and institutions. Early in the story,

Johnny O'Brien's father, a corrupt figure who advocates manly
violence against "sissies," Jews, and Negroes, seems like the
ideal father to Studs because he is a "regular guy" and an in-
fluential business man. In another of many instances, Father
Shannon, who is the voice of the Catholic Church to Studs,
assails godless universities, modern literature, and secular
thought. To Studs and his friends, his reasoning can only serve
to justify bigotry and violence.

We notice the poverty of alternatives that Studs's society offers
him. On the beach with Catherine, just before Studs's heart
attack while swimming in Lake Michigan, he comes about as
close as he can to self-recognition. He cannot understand the
causes of his plight, but he sees some facts clearly. Momentarily,
he is humble in his accurate self-appraisal. He feels weak and
powerless before his problems, and completely alone. His real
self is padlocked within. Seeing the sky and clouds above, he
"thought of what a big place the world was after all, and he
was sort of lost in it. He felt that he had always been like this"
(*JD*, 335). Having belittled Catherine in his thoughts, "he suddenly asked himself who the hell he was, wanting so damn much,
and thinking she wasn't enough for him" (*JD*, 335).

But Studs has not learned to base his habits upon his individual perceptions and innermost feelings. He usually acts
conventionally, and in imagination his responses become increasingly atrophied and trite. The self-revelation in this scene momentarily breaks through the crust of his stereotyped notions of
himself, only to fizzle out in his pitiful wish that "he were a six-
foot handsome bastard, built like a full-back, attracting the
attention of the crowd of bathers" (*JD*, 335). What might in
another have been the prelude to contrition and change, in
Studs is channeled away from action into one of the banal
images of greatness accepted in his culture. The impulse toward
truth and reform is dissipated in social cliché—the puny vestige
of a once rather vigorous imagination in the boy.

Similarly, *Studs Lonigan* is concerned with the creation of
social effects and institutions through character. Studs and his
friends patronize poolrooms, brothels, and dance halls. Their
sadistic jokes, the rapes and beatings, the instigation of race
riots are all to the point here. The book constantly returns to
the social disorganization or stagnation that is rooted in human

will. We see the process in the details of action when Jewboy
Schwartz is maimed by Studs's team, or where the restaurant
owner Gus fires Christy, his radical waiter, after receiving complaints from his customers. Because Studs is kidded about Lucy,
he leaves his friends from Indiana Avenue to join the tough
lads from Fifty-eighth and Prairie. He is accepted, life opens
up. He brings his natural leadership with him, and the gang
grows before our eyes.

Studs does not lack will, for a major point of the trilogy is
his constant and painful hacking at his humanity. As a boy, Studs
is often hopeful, imaginative, aware of his feelings, sensitive
to criticism—but outwardly he is already "hard." His standards
are naïve and unenlightened, yet he is sharply aware of the
difference between right and wrong. Morally, he is often at odds
with himself; he knows aspiration and guilt. Even toward the
end, his life holds potentiality for good as well as for evil. His
understanding grows in some respects. He is never really a
tough guy, and the slob never loses his conscience. Fundamental
to Studs's degradations and self-destruction are idealism and a
romantic flair. He wills to be tough precisely because the un-
predictable tender feelings and need for love are strong within
him and because toughness, he has learned, can be controlled
and can get results. Studs's "tough-guy" attitude is his bid for
self-fufillment. His obstinate pursuit of toughness, despite his
inner feelings and even—ludicrously—as a twenty-nine-year-old
weakling and runt in *Judgment Day*, shows the strength of his
commitment. Studs's misdirected will, in short, is always evident.

Knowing Lucy still likes him and facing her loss unless he
trusts his devotion, Studs nevertheless tries "to make himself
feel good by telling himself how tough he was" (*YL*, 170).
It does not work. He still loves Lucy, but he sticks to his ideal of
toughness. He is proud: "After all he was STUDS LONIGAN" (*YL*,
169). Another boy, Huck Finn, tried to make himself feel good
by attempting to do the conventional and inhuman thing; and
the effort did not work for him either. But Huck proceeded to
fool the Negro-hunters, and he later tore up the letter to Miss
Watson. Thus, in some of his loyalties and actions, Studs begins as a kind of truncated Huck, but he ends as his opposite.
Each is sensitive to the ideal of human communion, but Studs
learns not to will it: instead, he wills his own isolated hell. He

thinks he is "the real stuff" (*YL*, 152), but he denies his best impulses. Huck affirms his in action, but without full comprehension. He wills the godlike within, although in typical humility he thinks it is the devil. The difference is fundamentally a difference in character, and each boy's character may be regarded as a social product and as a human force affecting society.

Since Studs's society is more restricted and congealed than Huck's wide world, the results of man's evil are more easily compounded in it. Yet its corruptions are qualitatively no greater, and it too provides sources of spiritual strength and images of courage and love. Studs, for example, senses the integrity of Connolly, the Bug Club speaker from the University of Chicago; but his darkened will knows only how to vigorously condemn the university and all learning. One glorious afternoon Studs sits in the Washington Park tree with Lucy, "a prayer sprung into flesh" (*YL*, 115). But in the dark he steers Elizabeth Burns, the diseased "fourteen-year-old bitch" (*YMSL*, 67), to a spot on the ground "near the tree where he and Lucy had been" (*YMSL*, 81). Studs constantly wills his own victimization.

Studs is a dupe, but a vigorously cooperative one: a dupe of his time and place, and equally of his sensitivity and idealism. For his environment "takes" on him all too well because of his sensitivity and his desire for recognition. Lucy's feeling for him, Helen Shires's friendship, Davey Cohen's involvement with him, and Andy Le Gare's testimony that "Stutz Lonigan is the bes whitest guy of the older guy who hang around that pool roome den of iniquieties" (*YMSL*, 184)—all affirm his innate worth. Studs comes close to the average person who fails to realize his potential and descends to disaster. His ideal stature is best seen in his vision of felicity with Lucy, a quickly destroyed possibility but one destroyed through his own actions. His emotions and his mind atrophy as he progressively wills his destruction, from ignorance within and around him, until, in *Judgment Day,* regretful, somewhat aware, and more flexible than usual in his human relations, he finds that time has run out on him.

We know that *Studs Lonigan* did not arise from Farrell's desire to illustrate a sociological thesis or a philosophic position; the novel arose from very personal needs and powerful emotions. But the writing of *Studs Lonigan* was directly affected

by Farrell's creative use of ideas that he encountered in his
reading of the late 1920's. Among these were the concepts, expressed by leading American pragmatists, of habit, of will, and of
the interaction between the individual and his culture. By helping
Farrell formulate what he already felt emotionally, these ideas
strengthened his confidence in himself as an interpreter of his
past. They supported his tension-laden compulsion to explore
his experience more deeply by re-creating it in fiction. They
helped him to give fictional shape to the "tendencies"—a favorite
term of Dewey's—he had felt and seen at work in long years
of deeply absorbed experience. Above all else, perhaps, they
entered into his characterizations by providing him with a concept of the functional relationship of self to society.

II *Point of View and Cultural Process*

Studs Lonigan is the story of an aspiring person too responsive
to what only *seemed* best in his time and place. It is a vast
parable of the truth expressed in John 1: 1: "And the light
shineth in darkness; and the darkness comprehended it not."
Farrell's picture of Studs's culture includes both dark and light,
and the dark predominates to serve the author's purpose of
illumination and rejection.

The trilogy presents a neighborhood that is stagnant yet disintegrating. It depicts, within that neighborhood, the routine
actions and the stereotyped dialogue of the characters; the
stultifying influence upon them of basic institutions and of
cultural forces like the radio, the movies, and newspapers; and,
especially, the inner poverty of Studs's mind, which registers
much of the ugly cultural reality. Farrell has written in a letter
to E. Sculley Bradley of May 22, 1948: "In *Studs Lonigan* you
see boys, and also others, living in a world without ideas. The
most wonderful instrument in this world is the human mind.
The contempt for mind, the contempt for reason and thought
is implicit in the story of Studs." The physical setting is often
used to signify the enveloping darkness of mind. City streets,
vacant lots, dirty washrooms, poolrooms, and brothels—all suggest cumulatively the illiberal values of a way of life. The
realistic action and dialogue quickly become a flowing sign of
impoverished personality and social decay. Farrell's direct ex-

ploration of consciousness through the interior monologue bares the pulpy mind-stuff itself.

Farrell wanted to portray Studs's culture mainly from the standpoint of Studs's immediate experience. He desired the book to be so vivid that the reader would feel he was not reading a story but was intimately observing the course of a human life. The vividness would come from Farrell's objective method of "unfolding the destiny of Studs Lonigan in his own words, his own actions, his own patterns of thought and feeling"[3] to re-create a sense of what life meant to Studs. He hoped to avoid the direct authorial intrusion of commentary, generalization, and analysis.

The inarticulate Studs is, of course, remote from a Jamesian hero who savors his own fine awareness of life. Indeed, Studs cannot even tell a story, as Huck Finn can do. His consciousness is not penetrating, flexible, absorbent, or wide-ranging—part of the trilogy's point. Farrell adapted his method accordingly by not attempting to use Studs's mind as a filter for all the reality presented. In practice, Farrell's writing ranges from the interior monologue, which dips into reverie, fantasy, and dream, to a neutral recording of dialogue, action, and setting—writing focused on the externally present and scrubbed of subjective tinges. More typically, the representation of external reality, one frequently relying heavily upon dialogue, is colored by Studs's awareness, a merging of inner and outer worlds in varying proportions that helps determine pace of action, sense of time, and manner of character portrayal.

Farrell also creates patterns of experience beyond Studs's awareness. Occasionally, action unfolds in Studs's absence. The feelings of various characters temporarily color the writing, and Farrell uses the interior monologue for a number of his people, either in the interchapters as with Davey Cohen and Danny O'Neill, or in the main narrative stream, as with Weary Reilley and Frank Hertzog.

These shifts in viewpoint serve Farrell's ideal of objectivity by deepening our sense of what life means to Studs, and they add an additional dimension to Farrell's Realism. The interior glimpses into other lives provide both confirming and ironic perspectives on Studs, often in a fashion structurally useful. Paddy Lonigan's reveries near the beginning and the end of the trilogy, for example, form a framework that helps us to see Studs more clearly. Bristling with ironic implications, they demonstrate the identity of many basic values in father and son—the continuity of Studs's dark life with Paddy's difficult past and rather barren present.

In effect, the intimate revelation of numerous characters over many years anchors Studs firmly to the past and to his contemporaries in ongoing time. This method places him squarely in a particularized, sluggishly moving historical current; and it reveals him as individual but also as representative. It focuses upon temporal and spatial relationships. Thus the technique creates a sense of cultural process, of underlying tendencies affecting all the characters, though not necessarily in the same manner. This method enabled Farrell to observe a pattern of truth to experience larger than the pattern of Studs's awareness but consistent with it. Because we feel through Studs and still see him in context, we experience both the personal tragedy and the full implications of the flow of his life toward the trivial and shameful.

Farrell has written in a letter to Sherwood Kohn of December 10, 1960, that "Studs is a consumer who doesn't know how to consume," an insight into Studs's consumption of the standardized products of his culture, spiritual as well as material. To be sure, the trilogy expresses Farrell's interest in the effect of productive occupations upon human character, although less directly than *Gas-House McGinty* does. From 1919 until the early Depression, Studs is steadily employed as a painter, and Farrell occasionally pictures him at work. But we usually see Studs in his leisure moments, as a consumer—whether of movies, gin, platitudes, or time itself. In his critical writings Farrell has noted that twentieth-century American fiction reflects the growing dominance of a consumer psychology, a value-pattern that elevates consumption as a major good in itself and that denies inherent dignity to work, which is regarded as a necessary evil.

In this connection *Studs Lonigan* is a study in the misuse of leisure. It shows what happens to people when leisure is not used creatively but becomes the habitual, often aggressive reflex from equally habitual mechanical labor that satisfies few human impulses. Primarily, the story concerns the education of people off the job, during those times they supposedly can be most naturally themselves. The results are seen in the quality of Studs's life and in his death. As John Dewey phrased it in *Human Nature and Conduct,* a book fundamental in Farrell's thought when he wrote *Studs Lonigan,* education too often "becomes the art of taking advantage of the helplessness of the young"[4] by enlisting the will to form routine habits supporting the status quo, rather than intelligent habits directed toward re-creating the environment. *Studs Lonigan* strikes radically at both the ends and the means of a modern industrial society, as Farrell knew it in Chicago.

Studs Lonigan, in fact, is an accurate dramatization of the evils that were charged against an industrial society by the Southern Agrarians, who were voicing their criticism during the years Farrell was publishing his trilogy. Farrell was not influenced by these thinkers; his premises and theirs were poles apart, and their proposed solutions were remote from those implied in the trilogy. Still, the coincidence is close. John Crowe Ransom, noting that the good life depends upon leisure, wrote that "leisure depends on an establishment, and the establishment depends on a prevailing magnanimity which scorns personal advancement at the expense of the free activity of the mind."[5] Studs's parents, the children of immigrants, knew no "establishment" in America. A major purpose of Studs's education was to throttle the free activity of the mind—to reduce thought to stereotypes agreeable to those in positions of power in home, school, church, and business. And, what most of the characters in the trilogy lack in magnanimity, they amply possess in personal aggrandizement.

The Agrarian attack on industrialism is all there in fact or implication: the high value given to consumption, the concept of labor as an evil endured for material gain, the brutalization of our leisure satisfactions, the satiety and aimlessness of the modern man with little sense of vocation or pride in work, the atrophy of religion, the loss of a sense of mystery in nature and contact with nature itself, the withering of the arts and amenities, the insecurity of recurrent unemployment, and the lack of a humane tradition in society. Ransom called industrialism the contemporary form of pioneering, "a principle of boundless aggression against nature."[6] Studs, raised in the city, warred against his nature in order to fulfill the dream of the he-man as tough anti-egghead. As Farrell once wrote to Sherwood Kohn, December 10, 1960, Studs "is the aftermath in dream of the frontier days."

Virulent convention is widespread in Studs's middle-class society. At least as pervasive there as in George F. Babbitt's Zenith, it arises even more ominously from human predispositions than it does in Sinclair Lewis's novels. All of a piece are the materialism of the Lonigan girls, the respectability of the Dennis Gormans, and the narrow moralism and the commercial and religious pieties of many characters. Studs, who is romantic in his reveries, conforms in his actions. From his slightest sneer to his raging drunks, his defiance of respectability takes conventional forms. His "rebellion" is the other side of his padlocked feelings, the ugly reverse image of the secret, affectional self he suppresses.

The violence in the trilogy is a sure sign of the cultural ideal important to Studs. His aggressions, his acting the poolroom "tough guy," even his fantasies of himself as a "big shot" or as "the most powerful whale in all the seas and oceans" (*YL*, 145) shows Studs's faith in that ideal of rugged individualism evident in the rise of Paddy Lonigan from Shanty Irish to Lace Curtain Irish. As Studs phrases it in moments of confidence, he is fighting his way; in moments of discouragement, he is giving the lousy world a run for its money. The self-approval is constant. As he acts out his social role, or imaginatively reconstructs it, he is Lonewolf Lonigan with a "gat" in his hand, a hard guy who beats up on Jews and Negroes, a "goddamn . . . bull" (*JD*, 262) in sexual intercourse, a bonecrushing fullback, or a ruthless speculator on the stock market.

In effect, Studs, while yet remaining a true son of the culture, strips the clothing of respectability from the ideal of rugged individualism and thus finds himself at odds with respectability —with his sister Frances, for example, who is self-righteously disgusted with his drunkenness. He acts out the ideal of individualism in his human relationships more thoroughly than he can in his business life, where he is merely a flunkey to his father. As a dramatic character, Studs bares the violence and frustration in his competitive middle-class society. The naïve conformist to an illiberal ideal of individualism shows his society's potential for destroying both the individual and itself—and herein lies a fundamental ironic meaning of the trilogy.

When aggression and conflict are masked by respectability, they are accepted everywhere in Studs's culture. Human relations in church, school, family, business, love, and sports are riddled with brow-beating and open hostility. The potentially whole and flexible personality can become rigid and segmented: an insight of Farrell's true to his experience of the city and the one he found formulated in the writings of William James, Dewey, and George H. Mead. Later, in the Danny O'Neill books, Farrell provided a context for Studs's psychological world. In Danny he emphasized the human potentiality for creative growth arising out of social disorganization. But in the narrower frame of *Studs Lonigan,* although all is not black, Farrell extended the dramatization of social conflict, found earlier in the novels of Upton Sinclair and Theodore Dreiser, to the point where ideal elements, like an amiable temperament and the need for love, are themselves corruptible into loathsome patterns of emotion and violence. Where in *Studs Lonigan* do we find a buoyant Drouet or an untaintable Carrie with some wholeness of spirit as in *Sister Carrie,* or a mature reintegrated Jurgis, responsive to the ideal of human cooperation as in *The Jungle?* Danny is still on the sidelines. Frank Norris' McTeague and Trina, although not so infected by their city environment as Studs and some of his friends are, more closely parallel the corrupt destinies of Farrell's characters.

Studs's gang reflects the tensions and aggressions of his society; and these are visible in the gang's banter and practical jokes, its casual recreation, and its organized sports. Brutal sexual exploits and sexual taunts show one range of its aggressions. Its thefts and depradations are another, not unlike some business practices pictured by Farrell. The gang makes organized assaults on other groups, and it turns savagely on the marginal man like Davey Cohen unless, like Phil Rolfe, he has the strength to gain acceptance by making money. It shows little mercy to its own who, like Studs, fail and sink. Tough young Martin Lonigan beats up his older brother Studs, who becomes known as the brother-in-law of the once despised Phil Rolfe. Conflict between the generations and the races extends the picture of social war in *Studs Lonigan*. Farrell's focus upon the Irish Catholic community—people who live in tensions with themselves, with other nationalities, and with Protestants—gives the theme of conflict a special tang, sometimes tart or humorous.

More deadly serious are the stirrings of open class conflict plainly visible in the parade scene in *Judgment Day*, written when Farrell's perspective on his material had become more strongly Marxian. In this Depression novel we see social unrest swelling toward violence on a larger scale. A society seems about to disintegrate, although Studs cannot read the signs: the strikers and pickets, the apple vendors on the curb. Against this background of an order weakened by internal violence, we see Studs feeling sudden heart pains. He collapses on the day Paddy Lonigan loses his money in a bank failure. Personal and social disintegration become reciprocal symbols.

The disintegration Farrell pictures has deeper roots than doctrinaire Marxian theories of class conflict and the breakup of the middle class. The trilogy dramatizes a state of mind and soul shaped by conditions of life in the modern industrial city: its great size and its dense population of many types and races dynamically on the move and chasing the almighty dollar. The resulting frictions and insecurities, and Studs's adjustment to them, go a long way in explaining the meagerness of his life. For the city, requiring many specialized functions, encourages superficial or merely utilitarian relationships. It separates, it categorizes, and it reduces the personal to the anonymous.

City dwellers rarely engage each other's whole personalities. Except to the few, moreover, the city offers drudgery and monotony. It affords limited opportunity for a high-level integration of the self, yet it constantly and conspicuously displays the will-o-the-wisp of wealth and personal achievement. Because it undermines older forms of kinship and cohesion, it leads people to seek assurance and self-definition through the ingrown, segregated neighborhood or through the closely knit gang, or by way of the stereotyped ideas disseminated by urban newspapers and radio stations.

In the city, where people cluster for economic convenience, human needs are commercialized. A striking example of urban corruption, a symbol of city life itself, is the picture of Studs and Catherine attending the dance marathon—an episode whose very length and repetition has thematic relevance. Here for hours they escape the worse routine of their existence by becoming passive spectators of drugged dancers whose whole being is reduced to the meaningless desire to set an endurance record on the dance floor as jingling dimes and quarters are tossed in their direction.

Among the other characters who feel the disintegrating pressures of urban life is Stephen Lewis, a fourteen-year-old Negro. He is seen walking along Fifty-eighth Street where Studs once walked before his family moved to a new neighborhood. Stephen, who thinks of Eliza May Smith, has an "inward, self-absorbed expression" (*YMSL*, 412) upon his face. He gazes wide-eyed at the older fellows playing craps, and he steals butter from the corner grocery. This single touch is a measure of the distance between *Studs Lonigan* and proletarian fiction of the 1930's. It effectively shows the vitality of the cultural patterns, already seen in the middle-class Studs, among the economically and racially suppressed.

A major problem Farrell faced in his attempt to create a sense of what life meant to Studs was how to convey simultaneously a consciousness of the larger world of mature action—that background of tendencies and liberal values largely outside Studs's circumscribed awareness. Farrell set out to present experience subject to severe limitations, but he had to show Studs in perspective if his readers were to feel the full import of the waste in Studs's life and its consequences. Such a perspective also would show that the city provided possible avenues for Studs's humane development. In short, Farrell could not afford to omit the ideal element in Studs's culture even though his narrative point of view imposed difficult restrictions. We have already noticed how Farrell's handling of characters and viewpoint gives depth and range to his writing.

In addition, it should be observed that not all persons in the trilogy end as Studs does. Bit by bit Farrell builds up the life stories of many of Studs's contemporaries. Some die early and miserably. Others barely hang on, like Davey Cohen who becomes a drifter. Les Coady typifies others who are sunk in routine jobs. TB McCarthy and Red Kelly turn into well-fed politicians. Johnny O'Brien becomes a successful business man; Jim Clayburn and Austin McAuliffe become prosperous lawyers.

Such characters, who are seen intermittently and rarely from within, seem to fit into conventional social niches; and, in their own ways, they may be as conformist as Studs. Yet within the social order they are meaningful foils to Studs. Some of them pursue professional goals by civilized means, and their lives count in the world of adult affairs. Chance may play a part in the success or failure of all these characters, but determination and intelligent planning are usually important for those who succeed.

Farrell presents the ideal in life through ironic implication. If it is true that man's sorrow is the inverted image of his nobility, most readers of *Studs Lonigan* should be constantly aware of the levels Studs never reaches. The ignorance portrayed is so profound and many of the actions so shameful that they vibrate with a sense of their opposite. Apt examples are Paddy Lonigan's remarks on the value of education, Father Shannon's mission speech, Father Moylan's radio addresses, and the damning of the University of Chicago as an APA (American Protestant Association) institution. These episodes also positively suggest the presence of institutions and means in Studs's environment that disseminate information and promote learning and enlightenment. The trap Farrell sometimes fell into when using this method was what Clifton Fadiman noted about his writing—that the irony is too heavy-handed.

Farrell also evokes the ideal through the irony implicit in contrasting episodes and situations. Connolly, the intelligent, courageous Bug Club speaker who explains racial tensions as an outgrowth of urban growth patterns, saves a young boy from a trigger-happy cop; and we think back to ignorant Moonan, the poolroom cop and one of the gang, who callously shoots a boy, "just a goddamn alley-rat" (*YMSL,* 96). The enlightened is linked with the humane and courageous. Likewise, Farrell contrasts the hopeless and degraded end of Studs's life, as well as the hopeless and decadent Depression society, with the confident marchers Paddy Lonigan sees in his old neighborhood at the very moment Studs is dying.

Farrell includes in *Studs Lonigan* a number of characters who speak for enlightened opinion or who trust the life of feeling: Christy the waiter, Frank Hertzog, John Connolly, Danny O'Neill, the Red in the park, Mr. Le Gare, Abraham Clarkson,

Vinc Curley, Helen Shires, and Lucy. Farrell's use of newspaper
headlines, newsreels, radio programs and announcements, and
titles of current books, helps keep before us big issues and
movements of the day. As vitality, worth, and meaning fade
from Studs's life, Farrell never allows us to forget their presence
in the national life.

At times, but not frequently, Studs is in direct touch with
the excellence that might have given him the "something more"
he sought (*YMSL*, 132). Some of his friends continue through
high school and college into successful careers. Father Doneggan
and John Connolly briefly enter his life and awaken respect.
Lucy, in person or in reverie, always shows him the possibility
of another way. With Lucy in the park, Studs transcends himself
and feels identity with a finer life he senses around him. He
learns of a happiness unrelated to sneering self-assertion. Like
Sherwood Anderson's George Willard in "Sophistication," he has
a mature insight into some of life's limitations. What is good,
Studs understands, "couldn't last forever. That was the way
things were; they ended, just when they began to be most jake"
(*YL*, 113). Lucy, who brings out the best, the most mature, in
him, remains in his thoughts and fantasies to the end; and
around her image cluster his affections and religious impulses.
As a young boy, Studs daydreams of himself as a free and independent workingman nobly acting the man's part with Lucy.
In his dying delirium, Lucy says to him: "Be a man" (*JD*, 396).

As for Catherine Banahan, a warm and loyal person, her very
chatter shows a vitality, a healthy breadth of interest in life
unusual among Farrell's people. Next to Studs, she is perhaps
the best-drawn character in the trilogy. This is fortunate, for she
appears in the story when her influence is badly needed to
awaken in Studs whatever force he can still muster. For a short
time she calls out the tenderness, awe, and mastery in him. A
"decent" Catholic girl of lowly origins, she becomes pregnant
with Studs's child; as the book ends, she is used ironically to call
forth hatred and brutality in the family whose life she is per-
petuating.

In *Studs Lonigan* Farrell has allowed some room for the free
play of intelligence and good will in Studs's culture. Simple
social pleasures, human loyalties, and aspiring love—whatever
gives life its buoyancy and promise—are not ruled out. There

are characters who turn native abilities to account, whose emotions are not distorted or locked away. In the heart of the Fifty-eighth Street neighborhood live genuine radicals like Danny and Christy. Studs dreams other dreams and forms other habits, but alternatives to the course he chose were real possibilities in his life. The drift of circumstance, and especially depressing circumstance, by no means blindly rules all destinies in Farrell's Chicago.

The philosophy implicit in *Studs Lonigan* is not a simple determinism, nor is it even essentially pessimistic in outlook. For it is based upon the conviction that men have common emotional needs that can be fulfilled—the universal but plastic stuff of human nature. Farrell once wrote in a letter to Dr. Daniel Blain, June 1, 1951, that all people need "a sense of security, recognition, love and affection, an outlet for their impulses and energies, a sense of belonging and a feeling of participation in the culture of their times." In the process of living, habits formed to satisfy these needs are constantly being shaped and reshaped into an infinite variety of personality structures that affect human destinies.

As *Studs Lonigan* amply demonstrates, character is not merely the product of social institutions but has a distinct effect upon society: the human will, which acts either through rigid or through intelligently flexible habit patterns, shapes the environment for good or ill. When emotional needs are ignored or thwarted, as they are in Studs, the will may exert itself in aggressive and self-defeating ways. The trilogy condemns Studs's actions and their causes, but the condemnation would be flat and meaningless if separated from the animating belief that an individual can make his life humanly successful. The conviction that man's enlightened will can count heavily, if not always decisively, in shaping his life is central to Farrell's overwhelming picture of man's irrationality in willing what brutalizes and destroys. In *Studs Lonigan* there is appalling terror, but also belief in the power of reason and love. To see only the dark terror and to call it "pessimistic determinism" is to confuse the brilliant effect of Farrell's technique with the full range of meaning in the trilogy.

III *Symbolism and Theme*

Studs Lonigan directly communicates the cultural illusions and the isolation that stifle growth, the darkness and divisiveness that finally kill. It is a representative drama of man's self-destruction through his susceptibility to what is unreal in the sense of being spiritually blighting. Farrell's use of images, dramatic actions, and characters carries out this theme.

Images in the trilogy drawn from city and nature are solid, integral parts of Studs's Chicago that appear naturally as part of Studs's experience. They are causally significant in the story, and they focus much of the meaning implicit in Studs's destiny. Urban images are constantly used to suggest the limitations and lifelessness in Studs's character. Emerging through his awareness or in occasional objective descriptions, these images are as rigid and raucous as the crude stereotypes by which he lives. Studs the "iron man" (*YL*, 117), square cap on head and perched on the fireplug where two city streets meet, is a living symbol of his own restricted being. We note the "L" structure with its girders and steep steps under which the boys can look up to see forbidden sights; the sidewalks, curbs, and dusty streets; the vacant lots and drab buildings; the unpainted fences; the red lanterns hanging from railroad gates; the trains passing with "mechanical gruntings" on thin bands of steel (*JD*, 201); the darkened stores and "For Rent" signs in vacant windows. These make up the ugly, imprisoning physical environment Studs absorbs every day. They are metaphors of his mind and culture.

Likewise Farrell makes Studs's social actions symbolic of his culture. Studs's drinking, for instance, stimulates while it destroys. Studs shares a widespread belief in the fighting individual who sets himself against others and succeeds by domination. So liquor incites to aggression and lustful conquest; but Studs, unlike the porter in *Macbeth*, has not learned that liquor "provokes the desire, but . . . takes away the performance." Like the illusions Studs believes in, it whispers promises to his ear that it cannot keep. So, too, the ideology of aggressive individualism equivocates and deceives. As liquor produces insensibility and destroys the body, the ideology kills the social, thus truly successful, self.

Dancing, as used in the trilogy, is also culturally revealing. Studs and his friends go to Louisa Nolan's Dance Hall for easy pickups. They pay for a dance as they would for a trip to the brothel. Their dancing is a form of sexual competition and sexual aggression; "socking it in" is a foretaste of the lustful conquest to come (YMSL, 263). On the other hand, marathon dancing is purely commercial competition. In the spectators it arouses fantasies of sex and fortune compensating for their routine existence. Only Lucy's sorority dance calls out social abilities in Studs beyond being "a man" (YL, 191). But Studs has not learned to converse or to flirt; he is ill at ease and silent even with people sharing his background. Hopelessly out of place, he can only reassert his importance through the impulse to destroy. In this trilogy dancing helps us to understand the importance of money in Studs's Chicago and why some social patterns in Studs's life can shrink rather than enlarge his personality.

Farrell uses water imagery to reveal the inner Studs: not the "iron man," but the unique, unknown individual in need of love. Fluidity is constantly associated with Studs's deepest feelings and desires, with his ideal moments and dreams, and with important maturing experiences. His feelings for Lucy or Catherine are "melting," "misty," "seeping," "dissolving," or "flowing." The warm stream flows through him when he is close to Helen Shires. While he sits with Lucy in the Wooded Island tree, he feels "like he might be the lagoon, and the feelings she made inside of him were like the dancing feelings and the little waves the sun and wind made on it . . ." (YL, 114). In the trilogy water often suggests health, freedom, self-mastery, as when Studs swims in the "Y" pool and feels "removed from the world, clean" (YMSL, 235). Swimming in Lake Michigan stimulates his imaginative and reflective powers.

The same imagery suggests death, as David Owen has shown. Yet the seeming paradox is not real: if Studs gave in to his feelings, death indeed would be the fate of Studs Lonigan the tough guy; but to Studs the man of feeling, death subconsciously appeals as a release from his hell on earth. When Studs proposes to Catherine in Grant Park, near the flashing Buckingham Fountain and the pounding lake waves, the water imagery unites many of these associations. Here too, as in a few other places, the rolling lake waves suggest a source of strength Studs might have drawn upon had he trusted his instinct for love.

Washington and Jackson Parks, wooded and grassy, are settings for the bodies of water in *Studs Lonigan,* yet they are but a few steps from the busy streets. As Farrell uses the parks, they become charged with thematic significance. Studs goes to nearby Washington Park for many reasons—to sit with Lucy, to "goof around," to play hooky, to play ball, to box, to make love, and often to be alone. The park, which answers to many needs and moods, shapes itself to the conformations of his spirit. Whatever the dominant impulse, the park is where Studs can go just to be Studs Lonigan. There he can dream and act, or release the bottled-up feelings and confront his real condition. At the end of *Young Lonigan,* for instance, the lonely park is inseparable from the boy's state of mind: bare and windy, it is an uncomfortable refuge for the truant from school, and it reminds him of past happiness with Lucy and evokes moody questions. The imagery of the park best typifies Studs's complete self, the actual and the potential. Symbolically, it is the area of indeterminism in his character and destiny; yet, like Farrell's other symbols, it remains a solid part of empirical reality.

Other realistic elements also convey the basic attitudes that *Studs Lonigan* presents. The wind, often blowing, calls up fears of death in Studs. It helps dramatize his primitive Catholicism and conveys an emotional force rooted in Farrell's philosophic Naturalism. Because the trilogy is Farrell's oblique expression of faith in the values of the Enlightenment, it is appropriate that it employ the classic imagery of light and darkness. The writing is often a study in light and dark and in various shades of gray. Few colors enter the book, although we note the connection of blue with women that attract Studs sexually. Light and the sun, as might be expected, are associated with joy, warmth, vitality, and love, a complex of values also associated with the appropriate name Lucy. Far more prominent is the imagery of blackness; in scores of scenes the literal darkness of night, place, or costume parallels darkness of mind. The diction of some characters and their fantasy-images carry out the theme.

Blackness becomes linked with loneliness and estrangement, sexual and sadistic exploits, ignorance, and the presence and fear of death.

The importance of Negroes in the thoughts and lives of the white Irish Catholics makes possible an effectively ironic use of this imagery. What is "white" in Studs's idiom is often really "black," and the "Blacks" take on positive value because they are hated and mistreated for their efforts to find room to live. Also the deterioration and dispersal of a "superior" white neighborhood before the insweep of colored families is an index of relative social vitality. Yet Farrell does not sentimentalize the Negroes; Studs recognizes briefly that Negroes are happier than he is, but happiness and ignorance have no racial boundaries. Thus, we see the cycle of Studs's life being repeated by colored boys; and Danny O'Neill, working in an established Negro neighborhood in the heart of the Black Belt, feels "as if he were in a darkened corner of the world that had been trapped in a moment of static equilibrium. The light on the corner seemed only to emphasize the dreariness of the scene. Across from him was the box-like carburetor factory that stood now darkened like a menace of gloom" (*YMSL*, 369). Here slightly altered is the stagnancy and the ugly materialism of Studs's world.

Studs is Farrell's complete embodiment of his theme, which is dramatized partially in many other characters. When first seen, he is hostile; already he habitually denies the feelings that draw people together. His later affair with Catherine, a brief interlude of partial understanding, sets off the savage loneliness of his death, the final and logical expression of his life. As he is dying, the Lonigan family is shown in confused and bitter division. They are hostile to Catherine who carries Studs's child. The same note is repeatedly struck during the years between Studs's graduation and death. Studs loses touch with Helen Shires, who becomes merely a possible "notch in his belt" (*YMSL*, 168). He is wordless with his closest friend, Slug Mason. Even with Catherine he cannot put "the tumbling feelings" (*JD*, 204) into words. The inarticulate Studs, his tender emotions confined, is like an Anderson character; but, instead of turning into an innocuous grotesque, whimpering and hurt by life, he becomes a powerful symbol of social disruption. To use George H. Mead's phrase, the "generalized other" on which Studs relies for self-fulfillment is seductively and fatally restrictive.[7]

Farrell's treatment of sex is a variation on the same theme of destructive divisiveness as is the story of Davey Cohen. Even the gang members hardly communicate with each other beyond their stale banter. Chapter 20 in *The Young Manhood* makes the point well. Here are the prejudices and ignorant moralism of Fifty-eighth Street about Jews, Lesbians, Socialists, Americanism, and poetry. Counterpointed scenes show the lack of vital relations between Studs and others—Loretta, Phil, Vinc, Davey, Christy—and the utter boredom he feels. Yet he and they are beset with problems and need each other. The picture, which also includes the older generation clinging to respectability, shows a mechanical and atomized humanity. At the chapter's end, the doped somnambulist Hink Weber, ominously suggesting terror and madness, aptly symbolizes this condition. Farrell also takes pains to end each volume with a striking image of lonely isolation: Studs, without Lucy, is looking out on an empty street and searching for some anchorage; Studs, under the fireplug, is unconscious and deserted by his friends; Studs, dying in a whirling hallucination, is unreachable by those nearest to him.

From the initial illusions of the young "hard guy" mugging in the mirror to the dying hallucinations of the defeated weakling, Studs's life is a progress in unreality. What is reality to him and his gang increasingly takes on the aura of nightmare delusions about the terms on which life can be successfully lived. Advocates of "realism" and direct action, they become moving shadow figures in their world of fantasies. They see others under labels, not as individuals; and nearly everyone is consigned to a rejected minority: dagoes, micks, shines, polacks, kikes, mopes, punks, squirts, goofs, sheiks, radicals, atheists. They reduce love to sex. They show the immature self-absorption of provincials. The reveries of Studs and Paddy Lonigan contribute to this effect by showing them "sunk inwards," absorbed in their delusions and fantasies (*YL*, 18).

As Studs draws near his end, Farrell extends the range of delusion in his life and quickens the tempo of its appearance. In *Judgment Day*, which opens with Studs once again looking in the mirror, the pale and pasty face he sees no longer wears a sneer; but he still tries to convince himself he will outlive his friends and show the world. Studs's subsequent experience in early Depression days highlights his starved values and his fatal misreading of life. His initiation into the Order of Christopher, for example, is an ironic episode in false appearances. The initiation program is a hoax, but a greater one is Studs's belief in the grandiose organization. From the initiation Studs returns home to another dispenser of delusions, Father Moylan, the radio priest. He sees escapist movies like *Doomed Victory*. He views newsreels and reads headlines crazily mixing social tragedy and buffoonery. He hears insipid current songs ("Did you ever hear Pete go tweet-tweet-tweet on his piccolo . . ."). With Catherine, he watches the unbelievable dance marathons. Almost mesmerized, he follows the nightmare-like decline of Imbray stocks in which he has invested.

The world Studs knows becomes as delusive as Paddy Lonigan's diatribes against the Jew International Bankers, or Studs's rationalizations about his difficulties. Nor is the wider world beyond Studs's narrowing life lost sight of. For example, near Lake Michigan he overhears two university students discuss a Communist demonstration against Japanese imperialism. In this brief episode the reminder of the nearby university and of active world forces underscores his ignorant isolation, while the surging lake in the background suggests the vitality of nature. In this context, Studs appears as a wispy figure.

Increasingly, Studs moves like one in a dream. As his life becomes more hopeless, his dreams become more impossible and nostalgic. Although reality contradicts them, he never entirely relinquishes his dreams of sexual powers and financial mastery. Finally, as the future fades away even in vision, past and present merge and shift in his consciousness. On his last day of job-hunting the aura of unreality is built up in a striking crescendo effect. Studs's moods change rapidly. He applies for nonexistent jobs. He meets Mr. Peters, whose philosophy of salesmanship soars as far from reality as Studs's own sex fantasies. In desperation, he flees to the haven of a burlesque show and has an orgasm. His frenzied day, as void as his thirty years, has climaxed in exactly nothing and his life is spent.

In such ways Farrell rang the changes on the theme of appearance and reality and created a phantasmagoric effect arising from the realistic surface of Studs's life. Yet he adhered to the method that accurately uses the data of Studs's consciousness and environment. The method conveys in great density and with calculated pace the processes of Studs's experience in his particular time and place. It translates significant cultural tendencies of our century into terms of personal problems and individual destiny. It implicitly affirms love, rationality, and the development of the complete and social self: the human reality that Farrell believes can be renounced only at the cost of disintegration.

CHAPTER 4

The O'Neill-O'Flaherty Series—I

I *Scope and Genesis*

In *The Young Manhood of Studs Lonigan* Danny O'Neill, twenty-three, is a university student who works in a filling station where he studies while on the job. While he is reading Thorstein Veblen's *The Theory of Business Enterprise*, he feels an intense elation; his former convictions about life suddenly seem to be "so many maggots on the mouldering conception of God dead within his mind" (*YMSL*, 370). The revelation that old truths are mere delusion stirs him profoundly. Feeling personally liberated, he wants to destroy the old world of lies and to help create a new world of truth and beauty—and he wants to do it by being a writer. This same Danny, as a fourteen-year-old in Farrell's *Father and Son*, sits alone in his unhappy home on New Year's Eve, 1918. He is ostracized by his gang, which is having a good time at a party given by Roslyn Hayes, the girl Danny idolizes. Moved by yearning and hostility, he tries to record his feelings in his diary, but he cannot find the words. Farrell's five novels centering on Danny and his family show the growth of the child into the young man who finds the means to satisfy the deepest needs of his nature.

The central story of the pentalogy is of Danny's emergence out of a long foreground that is not unlike Studs's in some respects, for Danny wins his freedom from family and early environment and comes to the threshold of accomplishment. Having discarded supernaturalism, he wants to infuse humanitarian values into the existence that became "plain crap" (*YMSL*, 189) to Studs. In these books Farrell's imagination, one that had shaped Studs's earthly hell, turns to the origins of Danny's dream of "a newer, cleaner world" (*YMSL*, 371).

The Danny O'Neill series or, as Farrell prefers to call it, the O'Neill-O'Flaherty series, is a major part of his lifetime work. It includes: *A World I Never Made* (1936), *No Star Is Lost* (1938), *Father and Son* (1940), *My Days of Anger* (1943), and *The Face of Time* (1953).[1] The first four volumes compose the original tetralogy planned by Farrell in the 1930's. *The Face of Time* grew out of "Old Tom O'Flaherty," a short manuscript begun in September, 1951, about Danny and his grandfather, whom Farrell described in a letter to James Henle of October 1, 1951, as "a lovable old turkey." In time of action this novel stands first in the series and is integrated with it, even though it came years after Farrell believed he had written his last novel about Danny. Taking us back to the time Danny was five and six, it represents Farrell's sustained effort to recapture significant early experience in Danny's life.

The pentalogy selectively chronicles eighteen years and four months in the lives of Danny and his family. The action goes from 1909, when Danny is an insecure child of five, to 1927, when he resolutely leaves home and his college studies to become a writer in New York City. As in *Studs Lonigan,* the separate volumes cover periods of varying length; and the timegaps between the books range from eight months to over three and one-half years. *The Face of Time* spans twenty-one months from April, 1909, to December, 1910. *A World I Never Made* covers four months from August 27 to December 25, 1911, a period during which Danny begins his schooling. *No Star Is Lost* gives us the nine months between August, 1914, and April, 1915, when Danny is in fourth grade and turns eleven. *Father and Son* covers the five years between November, 1918, and November, 1923, a time including Danny's last year in grammar school and his high-school period. *My Days of Anger* resumes one year later and continues for two years and eight months, up to July, 1927. In this volume Danny gives up his night school and his job with the Express Company to attend the university. The action of the five books is drawn from ten and one-half years of the total span, and it falls on about two hundred and twenty days selected from the grand total of approximately sixty-seven hundred.

Because Danny O'Neill is the character closest to Farrell, it is a little surprising that the first volume in the series was Farrell's fifth novel and seventh book. Yet the idea for the series had simmered in his mind for years. He has stated that it led to his decision to become a writer, and certainly it was rapidly developing not long after that decision. Later, when he corresponded with Clifton Fadiman on June 24, 1929, about the work that became *Studs Lonigan,* Farrell described another novel in progress as "a tale of a boy in a Catholic high school of this city during the early part of the jazz age. It will deal with the innumerable conflicts resulting from the development of an adolescent sexualism, and the failing struggle to conform these impulses to the type of athlete idealized in this particular environment." The reference is chiefly to problems taken up in *Father and Son* eleven years later, although no mention is made of the father-son theme of the novel, or of family characters.

In August, 1931, Farrell unsuccessfully applied, as he states in a letter to James Henle of August 14, 1931, for a Guggenheim Fellowship to finance a trip to Ireland in order "to gather material for the first half volume of a . . . trilogy which will deal with two Irish immigrants who come to America, in the sixties, and whose sons and daughters raise the family status to that of lower middle class, only to be rather severely crushed in the tightening circumstances of capitalistic America." The plan at this time seemingly included historical fiction: a reconstruction of action in nineteenth-century Ireland and America. Danny is not mentioned, but we may be sure he still had a key role in the family's fortune.

While we should recognize the special status of *The Face of Time* as a late addition to the series, it seems safe to apply Farrell's 1936 statement about *A World I Never Made* to the entire pentalogy: "For years I have planned and replanned this work in my mind. I have mulled it over. I have gone back to recheck the material I have used. I have thought about it almost endlessly."[2] His long concern with Danny and his family is developed in short stories during the years he was writing *Studs Lonigan.* From the very beginning Danny, or one of his doubles, repeatedly appears in the writing. In July, 1928, before Farrell had published, he found himself broke and hungry on the streets of Indianapolis, where he had hitchhiked. Ironically, at that very

time he clarified the idea for his first published tale, "Slob." In
that story the unnamed nephew is Danny, struggling with his
drunken aunt. Danny also is close kin to Tim Kenny of "Autumn
Afternoon," the hitchhiker of "The Open Road," the narrator of
"Studs," and the kid of a "A Casual Incident." He shows up as
himself in "Boyhood" and "Helen, I Love You," to mention some
of his appearances in writing composed between 1928 and 1930.

The story "Boyhood"[3] is an excellent example of Farrell's
early exploration of the tensions lying behind the Danny O'Neill
pentalogy. Danny, now thirteen, can do almost everything better
than popular boys like Ralph and Billy; but the gang only tol-
erates him. Still, Danny knows he is not a "goof" like sissified
Jim English, and he works hard at being a regular guy. His
guarded affections have switched to Roslyn Hayes who, he has
heard, likes him. With high hopes for better days ahead, Danny
goes to a party. It ends in disaster for him—enmity with the boys
and disgrace in Roslyn's eyes. Defiantly, he stays away from
Roslyn's later party; but he thereby only increases his loneliness
and rejection. He wants to protest, to fight, "because somewhere
there was unfairness" (*Life*, 304). He walks alone in the bare
park and, like Studs with Lucy, has an unfortunate encounter
with Roslyn that makes their relationship worse. Hurt and bitter,
he turns miserably to Jim English, also wandering in the park.

The story is built upon a basic pattern that the romantic
Danny repeats many times in the pentalogy: under the shock of
reality, the boy's need for acceptance ends in disillusionment
and alienation, and as a misfit, he feels some shame and self-
blame; but, when the rejection by others is complete, the unfairness makes him vow to fight back and be a great man. The
story touches the core of Farrell's stubborn independence in the
face of rebuff and antagonism. "I'm walking this way, and I'm
gonna keep walking," Danny tells Ralph, who does not want to
be seen with him because "there's swearing in your house, and
your aunt gets drunk" (*Life*, 308). As the story ends, Danny
confides to Jim English that Rube Waddell is an idol of his. Rube
is already established in Danny's mind as the world's greatest
southpaw, who would not kowtow even to Connie Mack and,
when feeling right, "would sometimes walk three men, and then
call the side to sit around the pitching box while he whiffed the
next three batters" (*Life*, 284).

Slightly later, the Danny character turns up as Tom Kennedy
in "High-School Star" and Tommy McGrew in "The Hyland
Family." In some stories written before *A World I Never Made*
Danny appears only through the conversation of other characters
—a linking technique Farrell uses to relate different areas of
experience and to provide relative points of view toward characters and events. With varying degrees of admiration or dis-
approval, former friends speak of him as Al, a writer, in "Nostalgia"; as a New York advertising salesman in "Wedding Bells";
as a good athlete and an atheist in "Spring Evening"; and as a
Socialist in "Saturday Night." These particular stories explore a
way of life among lower middle-class Chicagoans that Danny
once shared, then outgrew.

Similarly, Farrell first explores the crucial University of Chicago experience, either with or without Danny as a character,
in early stories like "The Virginians Are Coming," "The Professor," "Angela," and "Clyde." The Danny character is seen in
"Accident" as a gas-station attendant named Tommy Rourke.
But it is the working day at the American Express Company, an
important part of Danny's life before he becomes a university
student, that Farrell particularly stresses in much of the early
fiction. In 1932 in Paris, Farrell wrote most of an Express Company trilogy which included *Gas-House McGinty,* a second long
manuscript burned in his 1946 apartment fire, and most of the
published stories about Willie Collins, Patsy McLaughlin, and
the others, including Danny, who worked the wagons or the
desks. Danny's father turns up as an Express Company teamster
in "Jim O'Neill," written in 1932, as does Danny's immediate
family. Mame Faherty in the very early story "Mary O'Reilley"
is an early sketch of Danny's mother, Lizz. Bridget and Susie in
"Two Sisters" are models for Lizz and Danny's Aunt Peg, and
the world of Peg's drunken binges is explored in "Meet the
Girls!" In his early stories Farrell also is interested in the neighborhood background and activity Studs and Danny share, and
he introduces characters from Catholic Church and business
who later figure in Danny's life. The O'Neill-O'Flaherty series
has a long background in Farrell's consciousness and fiction.

Not until February 5, 1934, did Farrell send Henle a rough
draft of part of *A World I Never Made.* Even then he delayed
serious work on his new book until March, 1935, when *Judgment*

Day was completed. At that time, as he related to James Henle on March 13, he began making additional rough drafts and keeping notebooks in order to "resurrect memory of things fading, and to get a slew of material organized." As he got into his work, he felt he was making a fresh start in writing; he was, he told Henle in a letter of August 25, 1935, sensing the world as he had in 1928 when he was "very itchy to get impressions . . . down."

By early 1937 Farrell knew his series would run to four volumes. He had outlined his work in progress, *No Star Is Lost,* and the two following volumes; but he still was uncertain how he would end the series and whether he would leave Danny in Chicago or take him to New York. Also he recognized the need to keep the style and organization of the unpublished volumes consistent with his approach in *A World I Never Made.* It is evident that from 1935 until 1943, when *My Days of Anger* was completed, Farrell increasingly centered his attention on Danny and his family. Four volumes of short stories, the novel *Ellen Rogers,* and the long story *Tommy Gallagher's Crusade* also belong to this period. Most of the publications, including many of the short stories written before 1935, focus on Danny O'Neill's Chicago.

In 1936 Farrell attributed his delay in writing the O'Neill-O'Flaherty series to a conscious act of self-discipline. He considered *Studs Lonigan* to be a preparation for the major literary effort to follow. One reason for the delay may have been that the new series posed intricate problems of characterization. Studs, the one truly major character of the trilogy, is not a complex person with a rich inner life and many personal relationships; his life is closely circumscribed and runs downhill to failure. Danny's life has more ups and downs before he finally moves rapidly toward independence after a vigorous rejection of the past. He has greater energy and potentiality than Studs and more interests. He absorbs a great deal and is emotionally entangled with many persons. He is surrounded by other major characters who are seriously engaged with problems of their daily existence.

Moreover, Farrell needed time to see Danny and his family clearly. He realized early that his closeness to these characters made it difficult to be objective in writing about them, and that his wisest course, as he said in 1938, was not to begin by licking his wounds. His full development of Danny, especially, depended literally upon his notable success with *Studs Lonigan* in the early 1930's. Before his personal past could assume clear significance and form, he had to see it from a present of unmistakable accomplishment; and his success confirmed the wisdom of his decision to write. Because his success showed he had been moving with direction, his past assumed meaning.

Farrell also delayed his full account of Danny's life because of an urgent need to write about Studs. As we have seen, Farrell identified partially with Studs who, during his short lifetime, developed in ways Farrell learned to condemn; but he represented tendencies not entirely foreign to Farrell's experience. Precisely because of the partial identification between the two, what Studs stood for demanded early denial; and, when Farrell had made the rejection inherent in *Studs Lonigan,* he was psychologically freer to unfold Danny's life.

In this respect, it is interesting to observe that, immediately after he completed his Studs trilogy, he wrote the story "Two Brothers." In it, Art McGoorty from Studs's environment shows the strength of character to overcome its worst features. Similarly, Danny's story provides a context and an alternative life course to Studs's destiny. In Danny's story Farrell's memories of his personal past are shaped into a fictional pattern of events. The events themselves often stay close to the remembered actuality, although much is invented; but the pattern is an imaginative construction of selected elements. It gives meaning and coherence to his past, and the dark background of *Studs Lonigan* helped him to bring out the new set of meanings.

II   *Centrality of the Series*

Farrell thought of the O'Neill-O'Flaherty series as a major effort that was more important than *Studs Lonigan* because he recognized the deep centrality of these books in his imagination and life work. In 1936 with only one volume of the pentalogy written, he called the series the "most important single group of literary works" in his lifetime program, a foundation stone for everything else. When the series is completed, he wrote, "it will place the author of these works within them, within the life that is portrayed. It will place the author on the same level as all his other characters. It will reveal the author as possessing the same frail mortality, the same human contradictions as those which he has revealed in his characters. It will unfold the genesis of this very plan of works of literature within the framework of these same works."[4] The Danny books also would enable him to plow once again and from a new angle into his Chicago experience. In this way, Farrell reasoned, he could see it and understand it more clearly; then he could get on with more certainty to other places and times as some critics in the middle 1930's were already suggesting that he do. But Farrell would not be hurried.

More nearly than *Studs Lonigan,* the O'Neill-O'Flaherty books approximate Farrell's plan of unfolding many American destinies within related social areas. Danny lives in more neighborhoods than Studs; he knows more people and has more jobs. He continues his schooling. He is part of two families in two distinct economic classes. He is often with his real family who live nearby and are always hard up. His father is a teamster most of his working life. Yet Danny lives with close relatives of middle-class means; not so wealthy as the Lonigans, they nevertheless have more pretensions to gentility. The pentalogy focuses on both of Danny's families. Its attention to the story of Peg and the prosperous Lorry Robinson also lets us glimpse a level of business and political activity rare in Farrell's writings. Moreover, the action ranges outside of Chicago, particularly with Al, the traveling salesman.

Although *Studs Lonigan* has many characters, one meager destiny dominates it. The pentalogy includes more characters, traces more careers, and presents several major figures with explosive emotional qualities. Essentially, it spans a three-generation process in which the laboring immigrant is transformed into the intellectual urban American. Unlike the trilogy and despite the limitation of individual characters, the Danny O'Neill books leave a sense of an open society. Revealing a broader spectrum of life than *Studs Lonigan,* they reflect Danny's drive toward liberation.

Danny himself is central in Farrell's writing and helps give it coherence. A "bridge" character, he links Fifty-eighth Street and a wider world in which intellect is important, whether in Chicago or in New York. Different as Studs and Ed Lanson of

Ellen Rogers are, each tends to see the future merely as the stage for individual self-assertion: for each, life is a personal contest with all others. Danny is also self-assertive, but he learns to see the future in relation to social forces and movements of ideas, as do other young men in Farrell's fiction. He develops powers of objectivity and analysis, and he follows through on his decisions. Thus Danny, showing regeneration and not disintegration, carries us from Studs to Bernard Carr. He is a transition character in Farrell's kind of "success" story.

The central imaginative impulse of Danny's story in the great bulk of Farrell's fiction of the 1920's and 1930's is evident in the early tale "Helen, I Love You" (*SS*, 3-9). Farrell wrote it in the summer of 1930, and his agent, Max Lieber, sold it to H. L. Mencken for a hundred dollars just before the Farrells arrived almost penniless in New York from Paris in April, 1932. A superior tale of a boy's yearning for love, Farrell called it "the story of a boy's adoration for a girl," or, more truly perhaps, simply "a story of a boy's adoration."[5] It tells of twelve-year-old Danny who recently has moved with his family to a new apartment near Fifty-seventh and Indiana Avenue, well away from the frustrating old neighborhood. Danny, who hopes he will be liked by the new kids, especially hopes that pretty redhaired Helen Scanlan will be his girl. He thinks she likes him, and they have spent one idyllic afternoon together. But tensions already are building up. Danny fears he may have lost Helen through his bashfulness, which one day kept him from going to the park with her. He remembers his spiteful defensive remark that had hurt her. Burdened by these worries, Danny is confronted by Dick Buckford, a good scrapper, in full view of Helen's house. Taunting and circling, the two boys dare each other to fight, but no blows are struck. Danny pretends that he beats up Dick, with Helen watching, and that she calls out to him: "Dan, I want to be your girl!" (*SS*, 9). Consumed with lonesomeness and fear, he indulges in lush fantasies as he walks at dusk in Washington Park wishing Helen were with him.

Danny's experience in this tale was essentially the author's. In an account of the tale's origin, Farrell wrote: "It is a story of telling the world, letting them know that this was me in those days. This is the boy I was as I really saw. This is what was inside of me. This is what wanted to be understood . . . I used to feel that if I were only understood by someone, loved as I wanted to be . . . life could be different."[6] But the story omits a significant part of the author's actual experience: egged on by Studs and his friends, Farrell, unlike Danny, had fought Dick in front of Helen's house and had won, gaining the admiration of the older boys. The omission was necessary to maintain the tone of the story. Yet in explaining it, Farrell wrote: "This may have been because I was at work, creating another image of myself as a boy—dividing myself into Danny, and giving a part of myself to Studs—which I was writing when I wrote 'Helen, I Love You.'"[7] In *Young Lonigan*, Studs whipped Weary Reilley in front of the Scanlans' house. The story also is a source of the tree scene between Lucy and Studs; and, as we have seen, the emotions it portrays are bound up with the evolving picture of Studs in the trilogy, just as they are germane to Danny's character in the pentalogy.

Danny's unhappiness is evident in the early tales and in the later series of novels. We read much about his social troubles arising from exceptional qualities his friends translate into "goofiness," or from a family not quite respectable by middle-class standards. We get an impression of Danny's spiritual restlessness as he is blocked at every turn in his search for understanding and recognition. The early tales bear out Farrell's statement to H. L. Mencken in a letter of March 21, 1946, that "My having become a writer is related to early frustrations and bewilderments, and to anxieties which accompany these." The remark clarifies the motivation behind all Farrell's writing, but it applies particularly to the fiction about Danny. In *Boarding House Blues*, Danny, struggling to become a writer, "wanted to find in himself some combination of words and ideas that would forever put to rest all that would not rest within him."[8]

More directly than Farrell's other fiction, the Danny O'Neill books are an adventure in self-understanding, for Farrell patterned Danny's development upon his own, and Danny's feelings approximate the "way it was" with Farrell during his formative years. The five volumes are the author's way of composing his life—of seeing it whole in all its early divisions and its ultimate direction. Considered as personal expression, these novels are his "means to find himself on earth" through self-exploration (*BHB*, 152). Danny's program in *Boarding House Blues* is "To

write and be a free man" (*BHB*, 153). After understanding
comes liberation, and literature is a satisfying way to rise above
necessity. "There is neither all freedom, nor all determinism,"
Farrell wrote in a letter to John Dewey on March 31, 1941. "But
literature is one of those realms in which man asserts his freedom, his spirit: in literature of a first rate order, man attains a
kind of imaginative freedom in which he asserts, implicitly, that
in his spirit, he will not be the slave of fate. He assimilates
tragedy, sorrow, bitterness." Clearly, much that is bitter and
tragic in Farrell's early life is written out in Danny's story.

III *The Two Families*

Danny's central position in the pentalogy cannot hide the
important roles of the adult O'Neills and O'Flahertys. These
characters, patterned upon members of Farrell's family, are some
of the most memorable figures in twentieth-century American
fiction. Farrell once wrote that anyone who called the O'Neill-
O'Flaherty novels a story merely about a boy growing up was
capable of confusing Mrs. Wiggs of the Cabbage Patch with
Becky Sharp of Thackeray's *Vanity Fair*.

Danny is the second child of Jim and Lizz O'Neill, whose
other children are Bill, Little Margaret, Dennis, Catherine, Bob,
and Arty. Jim, a hero in Farrell's fiction, is a proud, self-reliant
Chicago teamster of Tipperary stock who comes from Kentucky.
He is a man of unusual understanding and moral force. His
sensibilities are keen and his sympathies quick. A vigorous and
loyal father, he loves his children dearly, and he believes in
education, discipline, and hard work for them: as an unhappy
orphan, he had taught himself to read and write and had made
his own way in life. Jim dies in *Father and Son*, stricken by a
series of strokes ending in a paralysis of the right side. He is
Farrell's best workingman character, shown in his difficult and
sometimes tragic struggles in the early part of the century.

Like her husband, Lizz O'Flaherty O'Neill is a triumph of
characterization. She is a large woman with an aggressive and
salty personality, usually pregnant and always untidy and suffering from bad teeth. Her gift of language and invective is
equalled only by her mother's, and her devotion to Catholic
mythology and ritual is a consolation merging into delusion. As
wife, mother, daughter, sister, and neighbor, she is a central

figure in the pentalogy. In particular, she is the strong center of the O'Neill home; for, beneath her sloppiness, her violence, her churchgoing neglect of her family, she is a good wife and mother. She respects Jim and each of her children for what they are. Her love for them is deep-seated and elemental, not possessive and selfish. She is a woman whose native strength, under the stress of ignorance and poverty, shows in her capacity to endure and fight back. Because the O'Neill family is impoverished, Danny goes to live with Lizz's parents, Mary and Tom O'Flaherty, when he is three; and he is part of the O'Flaherty household for the next twenty years.

As a young man, Tom O'Flaherty left Ireland in a time of troubles in the early 1860's for America. His girl in Ireland, Mary Fox, the fastest runner at the Mullingar Fair, followed him. They were soon married in Brooklyn, not long after Lincoln was shot. After living in Green Bay, Wisconsin, they moved to Chicago. On Tom's slim wages as a teamster, these illiterate parents raised their children, Al, Margaret, Ned, Lizz, and Louise. Except as Tom lives later in Mary's vivid memory, he appears only in *The Face of Time* as an old man who is slowly dying of cancer and who is supported by Al and Margaret who are unmarried and live at home. Fundamentally, Tom is not at ease in America and still yearns for Ireland. He is gentle and understanding, but his dependent existence is a heavy burden to him. He is merely Danny's nursemaid and Mary's errand boy. Once a vigorous worker and a fun-loving companion to his children, he is closer to Jim O'Neill than to anyone else. He is racked by abdominal pains and by fears, but keeps his spirit to the agonizing end. Lying in the hospital not long before his death, he is as capable of lyrical memories of his Mary as of the wry observation: "They were all born to boss in me wife's family" (*Face*, 326).

Top boss that she is, his wife Mary is a dominating character throughout the pentalogy, and she is one of Farrell's finest creations. Tough and resilient at the core, shrewd and resourceful, the old woman never loses her zestful will to live and to control. She knows that "a man must be said by his wife" (*Face*, 329). Despite her age, she retains a youthfulness and a naïveté that never lets us forget she was once a pretty young thing "running the bush in the old country," a girl who did not go to school,

but who "met the scholars" (*Days*, 366)—and undoubtedly sub-
dued them. Like her daughter Lizz, Mary is a throwback to
peasant Ireland; many American ways remain foreign to her.
She lacks subtlty of understanding, but her range of humanity
is most impressive, from her sly deceptions to her deeply felt
loyalties and loves. In her old age as Danny's "Mother" in place
of Lizz ("Mama"), she takes on a difficult role with genuine
affection and wisdom, and with the fierceness of a tigress.

Al O'Flaherty, the oldest of Mary's children who lived beyond
birth, is the financial mainstay of the O'Flaherty household, a
traveling shoe salesman like his brother Ned. Al is a small man
and was a serious, obedient boy. His early recoil of shame from
the poverty and violence in his home ultimately turns him into
the good provider who cares more for discipline and decorum
than for the wishes of others. A rigid and essentially immature
personality, he can act kindly but also cruelly toward his
nephews and nieces, just as he used to beat his sisters to enforce
harmony in the family. Al, a ritualist who worships propriety,
has little understanding of others. Yet more than any other
O'Flaherty, Al in his twisted way represents the yearning for
the good life, and the will to make it prevail. He will force
others to be happy. Like all his family, he suffers from alienation; but perhaps his alienation is the most lonely of all because
of his inflexible preference for principle over people. His genuine
strength is proved at the end of *My Days of Anger*: undaunted
after he loses his life savings and his job, he courageously
makes a fresh start. Al has some of the unquenchable optimism
and grotesquerie of Mark Twain's Colonel Sellers.

Al's brother Ned appears rarely in the story until he returns
childless after his wife's death in 1916 to the family home from
Madison, Wisconsin. Ned, an agreeable person who is weak and
self-indulgent, is less successful than his brother. He lacks Al's
imperiousness but is just as capable of unreasoning cruelty; and
his powers of self-deception are greater than Al's. The thought
of death is so fearfully repulsive to Ned that he is an outspoken
convert of New Thought, convinced that positive thinking can
show evil and disease to be illusory. Louise, the youngest daughter, is, like Ned, a relatively minor character among the O'Flaherty children. When barely twenty-one she dies of tuberculosis
soon after her father's death. A beautiful, auburn-haired girl

filled with the desire to live, Louise becomes increasingly melancholy and introspective as her disease progresses. Although she is comparatively colorless when compared to her sisters, she is of primary importance in Danny's early emotional life.

Margaret, or Peg, O'Flaherty has the vividness and long life that Louise lacks. Like Al, Peg does not marry; and she helps to support her parents by working as a hotel cashier. Peg, intelligent and attractive, is capable of thoroughly enjoying her family and assuming domestic responsibility; but she is the family's greatest problem. Her prolonged drunks, her thefts, her love affairs, her attempts at suicide, her constant self-lacerations, and her explosive outbursts keep the family in turmoil. Her troubles may be traced to her childhood experience of violence and repression in the family, particularly from Al's domination. We come to understand that her drinking and her promiscuity are her way of escape and of humiliating the decorous Al. Her prolonged affair with Lorry Robinson does not bring her the love and release she needs, for it is based only on sex and exists more in her frantic hopes than in the infrequent and furtive assignations Lorry keeps. Although Peg wallows in self-pity, her torture is genuinely acute, the subjective counterpart of her orgiastic actions. At the end of *My Days of Anger,* Peg resolutely assumes domestic responsibility when her mother dies; but, knowing Peg, we feel certain the old patterns will persist, even in exaggerated form.

Following his practice in *Studs Lonigan,* Farrell carefully locates his two families in their Chicago setting. In each of the first three volumes Danny and the O'Flahertys live in a different apartment; and each place is about two blocks removed from the former dwelling. At the end of *No Star Is Lost,* they have moved again, this time six blocks away. The new home is near Fifty-seventh Street and Indiana Avenue in Studs's neighborhood, and the significance of the move is marked by the early meeting of the two boys. Through the last two volumes the O'Flahertys live in the same neighborhood on South Park Avenue near Fifty-eighth Street. Their apartment overlooks Washington Park and faces the distant towers of the University of Chicago. Their successive removals are to the south and slightly to the east. The O'Neills follow a similar pattern. During the first two volumes they live on La Salle Street near Twenty-fifth Street, then in the little cottage near Forty-fifth Street and Fuller Park, and, beginning with *Father and Son,* in their hot water apartment on Calumet Avenue near Fifty-ninth Street. The moves of the two families reflect a slow rise in their prosperity.

But neighborhood setting does not play a crucial role in the lives of the adults, nor is it as important to Danny's development as to Studs's. Danny as a small boy is carefully sheltered, and he never finds a group to which he can truly belong. His development follows spiritual turmoil arising from family discord and social inacceptability. His struggle is essentially to discover himself and to breathe the free air of a spacious world. He moves slowly toward this goal, away from the stifling values and their neighborhood counterparts that smother Studs. Moreover, in following the lives of the O'Neills and the O'Flahertys, much of the action takes place in the home or miles away in the place of work. Consequently, we get a stronger sense of the confining apartment or job than of the confining neighborhood. But Danny breaks from home and work to the more rarefied university atmosphere, as Studs never broke from what bound him. For these reasons the city is more broadly present in the Danny O'Neill pentalogy but less immediately and fatally than in the earlier trilogy. The concrete images of the outdoor urban world so effectively employed in *Studs Lonigan* are not so evident in the later work.

Nevertheless, the O'Neill-O'Flaherty books continue Farrell's indictment of urban conditions; social protest is still part of his complex motivation. The two works have a common cultural reference. Each sees, as Farrell stated in his letter of October 10, 1942, to James Henle, deprivation and broken lives as an outcome of "a system marching to its own destiny," as the human cost of urban America's growth. "Get away from the lake front," Farrell wrote to Ralph Marcus on August 10, 1943, "and what a vast slum Chicago is . . . you see all those streets, streets which you knew at different ages, terrible blocks of buildings, red, gray, yellow and brown brick with dreary little ornamentations, and think of the life lived inside these bricks, the lives sunk in banality . . . the endless pressure for money, place, advancing, the spiritual privation of these people—this world to me of Studs, of the O'Neills, McGinty . . ." In the pentalogy Farrell wanted to show as he indicated in his letter to

Meyer Schapiro, June 24, 1945, what this "garbage dump" of a Chicago meant for the O'Neills and the O'Flahertys. They too felt the fierce individualism of the streets in their very homes. Much that was creative in them suffered distortion or suppression—we think of Jim O'Neill's love of poetry. The inner life was ritualized to conform to patterns of authority in commerce, business, church, and human relations. Farrell remembers that he once felt it was a sin to dream or to think.

Because these relatives suffered and were close to him, Farrell is interested in his adult characters for their own sakes and not merely as adjuncts to Danny's growth, although they are that. He sees them as Irish Americans and as autonomous human beings. In 1936 he stated: "The people I have written about are the people of my race. Their historic past is my historic past" (Typescript A, p. 4). Danny must reject these people before he can be independent; Farrell, as distinct from Danny, accepts them with their limitations. He expressed a fundamental attitude of the pentalogy in writing: "I do not detest these people. I do not seek to insult them by saying that I pity them. I love them. I believe that they are fundamentally good and decent. I detest the conditions which have maimed, twisted, and frustrated their lives. I want others to detest these conditions" (Typescript A, p. 2). The implied faith also lies behind *Studs Lonigan;* but, while the trilogy rejects a way of life Farrell felt some identity with, the pentalogy basically accepts a people whose life he transcended.

In 1935, Farrell considered "The Fighting O'Flahertys" as the title for the first volume of his new series. On March 14 he wrote to Henle: "I heard of a sign the Norman conquerors left in the Aran Islands after they met the clan of O'Flaherty, which reads—From the fighting O'Flahertys, good Lord deliver us." The fighter Danny, who delivered himself from the O'Flahertys, thus proved himself one of them. Expressing more than personal release and social criticism, the O'Neill-O'Flaherty books are also Farrell's act of piety toward his family, people of ancient Irish heritage. When he returned to Chicago in 1945 to see again the dirt and grime and smoke in which his people lived, he wrote to Meyer Schapiro, June 24, 1945: "It is as if so much of their natural feeling were forever lost in these black palls of smoke . . ." The pentalogy is an effort to recapture those feelings, to make the members of the family live again by showing exactly what they were and just how their lives went in the city they helped to build. To be true, the picture had to include relentlessly their violence and weakness as well as their affection and will to live. Only so could it be an honest tribute to those who had dreamed of a life of greater dignity than any they ever knew.

CHAPTER 5

The O'Neill-O'Flaherty Series — II

I Danny's Story

The inner story of the O'Neill-O'Flaherty books is the emergence of Danny, the incipient artist, from his early environment. The adults surrounding him intimately affect his growth and are bound to him by strong emotions. Since their characters are relatively fixed by 1909, the family is a fairly stable human backdrop to Danny's story. We measure him against it as he changes from a dependent child among towering adults to the young man whose educated perception reduces them to true scale.

Danny's development follows from first to last a consistent pattern. When he was scarcely three, as we have seen, he was taken by his Uncle Ned to stay with the O'Flahertys while his mother was having Little Margaret. Two weeks later Jim O'Neill brought him back home, but Danny screamed convulsively until Jim was afraid he would die. Jim took him back to the O'Flahertys by streetcar at two o'clock in the morning, holding him in his arms and trying vainly to quiet his sobbing. When they reached the grandmother's apartment, Danny stretched out his arms and said: "Mother, put me to bed!" (*World*, 70).

This traumatic experience sets the pattern of Danny's future relations to others, from the time we first see him, seeking acceptance from his grandfather and from Father Hunt, to his grief at Mary O'Flaherty's death eighteen years later. The boy, who feels excluded by his mother (Mama), in turn rejects his parents and transfers his affection to his grandmother (Mother). The experience lies behind Danny's belief that Mama does not love him but that Mother does, and his wish that Mother were his real mother. It helps explain why Danny, ashamed of his mother Lizz and revolted when she nurses her baby in his presence, feels physically attracted to Mrs. O'Flaherty, to Aunt Louise, and even to Aunt Peg: for the two sisters also stand as mothers to the boy.

The traumatic experience also is like a well of fear in Danny. It helps account for later anxieties and for his nervous sickness when he visits his real parents. Farrell's appropriate first choice of a title for *The Face of Time* was *A Legacy of Fear*. The germ of the boy's strained relationship with his father also lies within the experience, as does Jim O'Neill's bitter realization that Danny's preference for the O'Flahertys is a denial of himself and Lizz. With her ever increasing brood, Lizz can accept Danny's becoming the "son" of her closest relatives; but Jim puts the blame for the alienation upon the O'Flahertys and damns them and the economic hardship that robbed him of a son. The imaginative impact of the experience upon Farrell appears, as we have seen, even before the Danny O'Neill series: Studs Lonigan's last coherent words in the trilogy were: "Mom, I'm sick. Put me to bed" (*JD*, 388).

Because Danny is the son in two families, his position in each is ambiguous and a subject of contention between the adults. He seeks an identity denied him. Other boys, he knows, lead normal family lives; but he is "different," is pulled two ways, and never knows for sure where he stands. Although he is taken into the fiercely possessive O'Flaherty circle, its love can quickly turn into hostility or temporary indifference. Fundamentally, the O'Flahertys use him to satisfy their needs. Danny thus knows from the inside what it means to be an outsider—even doubly an outsider. The child's consequent bewilderment is inevitable, for no fewer than three men and four women share the parental relationship to him: besides the real parents and the two grandparents, there are the two aunts and Uncle Al.

Family quarrels over Danny or over Aunt Peg's affairs swirl around him. They are burned into his memory and increase his anxiety and lonely unhappiness. His false position keeps him insecure all through his youth, and it intensifies his search for understanding. It also quickens his desire for a wholesome directness in his personal relations. When these satisfactions are denied him, his reaction is likely to be sharp, rebellious. His revolt takes many shapes: drunken insults to Sheila Cullen who has repulsed him, athletic achievement in high school, and intellectual status at the university. Whatever its form, his rebellion is intended to assert his importance and independence, to help him leave the past behind and to move on to the new friend, the new neighborhood, or the new belief.

This pattern is the driving force behind Danny's development throughout. We see it, for example, in his love and rejection of Aunt Louise, his screaming defiance of Uncle Al's injustice to him, his break with his young friends at Crucifixion School, his troubles in dating and with his St. Stanislaus classmates. As a senior in high school, Danny summed up his troubles this way: "he was considered a goof by the fellows. He couldn't be one of them. They didn't take him seriously. Girls didn't take him seriously. . . . He wanted to be popular and he couldn't. He wanted to be somebody, and no matter what his feats were in athletics, still he wasn't treated like somebody. . . . Again and again in his life, the same thing always happened" (*Son*, p. 480). In *My Days of Anger* the pattern remains the same, but a decisive new element is the college education that provides a fresh perspective on his origins, a new objective, and the weapon to make his revolt effective.

True to this basic pattern, Danny gradually takes on substance and color: Farrell is as interested in showing processes of growth as in delineating the end result. *The Face of Time* reveals an impressionable child overshadowed by adults already set in their ways. In many respects Danny is fortunate, and he has happy moments; yet he exists in a kind of lonely helplessness. The boy is quick to feel, and he sees with honest clarity. He absorbs a great deal. Already he has hurts smoldering inside, and he is beset by anxieties. He is often afraid, particularly when the grownups fight; and he learns the pain of loving when love is not returned. Also he knows the willful unpredictability of adults who exact strict obedience of children; through fear and punishment, the idea of authority is internalized within him.

But Danny knows nothing of Al's shame as a child, of his aunts' bitter memories of cruel discipline, of Peg's unhappy love affair, of Louise's preoccupation with her coming death, or of Jim's hard past. Nor does he understand his brother Bill's need to boss him, or Jim's alternating tenderness and temper toward him. Sensitive to others' feelings for him, confused in his loyalties, reaching out for affection, keenly aware of unfairness, he is

like a chip on a torrent of adult emotions. The Danny O'Neill of
My Days of Anger who wants to be a free man and a writer is
already visible in the small boy who wants to be a grownup so
"he could do what he wanted to do and not have to always do
what he was told" (*Face*, 256-57).

In *The Face of Time* Danny is effectively contrasted to his
dying grandfather, Tom O'Flaherty. One is leaving life in pain;
the other, becoming aware of life and its final meaning of death.
Each in his way is helpless, and each has strong intuitive feelings.
But Danny is too young to formulate the future or to understand
the past. Old Tom looks back upon his life and ponders its
mystery, trying to see what it has meant for him, a stranger in a
new land. Danny, so new to life, comes to see what death is and
that love is powerless before it. His introduction to some of life's
profundities is direct and searing: "And Father didn't move.
Danny stood in the center of the parlor looking with transfixed
eyes at the corpse of Old Tom, and he heard whispering voices
in the dining room, low agonized sobs of his Aunt Margaret, and
then the noise of a streetcar going by on Indiana Avenue" (*Face*,
366). This ending appropriately shows the last meeting on earth
of the family's Old World source and its most vigorous New
World expression. The boy will carry the family's struggle into
new regions of endeavor; but he will never really escape the
corpse of Tom, the whispering voices in the dining room, and
the noise of a streetcar on Indiana Avenue.

The seven-year-old Danny of *A World I Never Made* is no
longer the dependent baby; but, as Farrell notes in the introduction to this novel, he is still the anxious little boy with many
fears, still something of a stranger who feels homeless. He remains closely tied to the family, but outside interests that eventually break family control begin to enter his life. In school and
on the streets he broadens his experience of the world he never
made. His active interest in baseball is a good example of Farrell's use of common materials to suggest the dynamics of his
growth. Because the grownups consider Danny's expert knowledge of the game as precociously cute, it wins their praise and
approval. More importantly, it secures a place for him in the
adult male world, for baseball is an interest shared by Farrell's
men and boys. Baseball also offers him a kind of experience
he can control—on the diamond and in his imagination. It enables

him to fuse reality and fantasy into a completely satisfying whole. What Farrell once remarked about himself is true of Danny: the campaigns of the White Sox become part of his struggle for confidence and status. The inclusion of the long account of Ed Walsh's "no-hitter" early in *A World I Never Made* may be formally unjustifiable, yet it dramatizes a significant area of Danny's experience.

Danny's rising interest in sex is an early instance of the honest portrayal of juvenile sexuality in American fiction. To seven-year-old Danny sex is perhaps not so engrossing as baseball, but its insistent upsurge in his thoughts is psychologically true. His curiosity about girls and babies is a channel for his growing imagination and is the early stage of his later discouraging efforts to find favor with girls. Danny's sexuality, like his brother Bill's fascination with the O'Flahertys' running-water toilet, is also social commentary. For Danny's guilty knowledge is partly an effect of crowded urban intimacy. Through open bedroom doors he sees his aunts nude; he cannot escape Peg's intrigue with Lorry Robinson; his knowledge of babies comes from Bill, who has learned the facts of life in the crowded O'Neill home; he plays doctor with Little Margaret. Farrell's knowledge of Freud may have helped him decide to include such scenes, but the remembered experience is more important to the imaginative reconstruction.

Danny's interest in sex is a minor development compared to other growing powers that foreshadow the idealist and intellectual. His loyalty to his family is marked in his fight with Arty Lenehan and in his defense of the injured Bill against Bull Young. Danny's sense of honor and his respect for the truth are seen early in his talk with Sister Marguerita and later with the department-store Santa Claus. Similarly, his sense of injustice grows sharper; and strong feelings of guilt involve him ever more deeply in the complexities of right and wrong, as when Bill makes use of him to further his stealing and smoking. His sensitivity and childish clear-sightedness lead him to perceive a few simple contradictions within his experience and even to question accepted ideas of God. The first glimmerings of logical powers appear; a judiciousness is evident when he wonders why kids will perversely argue against the facts. Together with his occasional cleverness and his capacity for faith, these qualities

establish Danny as exceptional. Yet they are intimately connected
with the blunderings, weaknesses, quaverings, and missteps
appropriate to an unsure seven-year-old. The result is a balanced
picture of a boy. Danny is rarely, if ever, sentimentalized.

As a preadolescent in *No Star Is Lost,* Danny experiences
mounting tensions and bewilderments. He lives more in a public
world than before; his fight with Stewie, the escapade with Bill
at the Penny Arcade, the "shagging" at Dunne's candy store, his
excursions to the ball park, his ice-skating—these are typical of
new experiences often accompanied by inner conflicts and
trouble with the family. Danny's desire for acceptance by his
classmates grows stronger as he sees more clearly the difference
between his family and theirs. His visit to Perc Dineen's well-
ordered home is a revelation, and trouble between the O'Neills
and the O'Flahertys heightens his fear of disgrace.

His growing sense of insecurity because of his family attains
substance as Farrell explores in some detail the lives of his
brothers and sisters and the preoccupations of the adults. Peg's
guilty remorse leading to her drunken suicide attempts, Mrs.
O'Flaherty's spunky communion with Tom in his grave, Lizz's
epic fights with Mrs. Connerty, and Al's lonely reaching out to
Dr. Geraghty sound typical keynotes in a book rich in humor
and pathos. All such scenes help to fill in the background of
Danny's expanding world. We see more clearly the hierarchy
of authority he must eventually confront and reject—the chain
of command running from God through parents and relatives,
priests and nuns, policemen, grownups, and older boys. But by
the end of the book, as his removal to the new neighborhood
shows, Danny still knows only how to escape and not how to
dominate.

As Danny goes through eighth grade and high school in the
years covered by *Father and Son,* his troubles grow. He resolves
a major conflict when he decides not to study for the priesthood
at the seminary. At St. Stanislaus High School, he achieves a
certain formal standing as student and athlete; but, as Farrell
wrote to Laurence Pollinger on March 10, 1939, there remains
"an irreducible core of inadaptability to the world he knows."
He fails with the girls, he muffs chances in sports, and he cannot
win complete respect or good fellowship from his classmates.
His best plans end in anticlimax or ineptitude, and he secretly

burns with humiliation. He is bitter at his failures and his poor prospects, but he also feels guilty for continuing his schooling while his father is dying.

Late in his senior year Danny is at lowest ebb—castigated by Jim, laughed at by his teammates, spied on by Hiram the Wolf at the Express Company, injured in his work, and torn by savage self-deprecation. At graduation he feels his high-school life has been wasted. In short, he has neither the money nor the personality to play the role he desires. His efforts to fit the stereotypes of his surroundings are building the inner pressures that eventually erupt in the revolt he cannot yet conceive.

Thus Danny in high school is still the unsuccessful conformist. He staunchly defends the Catholic faith; he believes Nature is sin; he goes in for popularity, fraternities, activities, and occasional ostentatious drinking. At one point he renounces study and gives up his grandiose but vague professional ambitions for the ideal of business success. He tries to make himself believe that he will be rewarded for doing a boring job carefully. But the signs of the future nonconformist are unmistakable. His early susceptibility to "the call" (*Son*, 136), his sporadic sense of destiny despite failures, his inability to keep his mind on routine work, his ineradicable "goofiness" testify to an unchanneled creative drive. Moreover, his inclination to speak the truth at inopportune moments and his moral seriousness, seen in the rudimentary analysis he brings to religious discussion, show him blindly groping for the values of the courageous thinker. As *Father and Son* ends, Danny still lacks critical awareness, but the ties to his environment are wearing thin. He is pretty much on his own, directly engaged with his destiny. He is beginning to appreciate the tragedy of his father's life, which is, in some respects, an example for him. Although he cannot yet understand the full implications of Jim's death, the ground is laid for his condemnation of what destroyed his father.

Danny's maturing character is also defined by the picture of Jim in *Father and Son*. For Jim is Danny's spiritual father as well as his real one—and the full realization of this fact illustrates the added dimension of meaning that comes from considering the five Danny O'Neill novels as a unit. Jim has the sensitivity, courage, determination, level-headedness, and drive that Danny will need for his success. Of all the characters, Jim as a strong

union man is most closely allied to a dynamic social force.
His experience has taught him the meaning of class differences
and class relationships. He trusts in his own two arms rather
than in the power of prayer and in the intervention of the saints
or the Virgin. His deeply felt love for his family and his courageous hates are qualities his son will need to depict characters
in a world they never made. Thus, in its essentials, Jim's life,
although it ends in physical and moral deterioration, is a pre-
diction of Danny's career. Jim used what means he could command to wrest happiness and order from his world; and, unlike
Al, he did not do so at the expense of others, thereby causing
more unhappiness and fear. Danny will seek the same end
through other means, on the level of intellectual and creative
endeavor. Ironically, he begins to recognize Jim as his true
spiritual father only after Jim's death.

As *My Days of Anger* opens, more than a year's drudgery for
the Express Company drives Danny back to study, first in night
school and then at the university. Initially, he is still the con-
ventionalist, and also a pious bore. He mouths platitudes and
has a fondness for romantic notions. His professional ambitions
are still orthodox and dull. But Swinburne and Shelley set words
singing in his head; and exciting ideas about the potentialities
of human development, expressed by T. H. Huxley, Matthew
Arnold, Cardinal Newman, and Walter Pater whet his appetite
for distinctive accomplishment. A reading of Sinclair Lewis'
Babbitt undermines his salesman's philosophy.

During Danny's second and third quarters at the university,
the old gods begin to tumble rapidly; for the tensions of many
years now find release through knowledge. The reading of
Henry George, Thorstein Veblen, Nietzsche, and Theodore
Dreiser hastens the creative upheaval. He quickly sees through
"college spirit." He begins to lose social fears and cheap social
ambitions as he grandiosely identifies with Napoleon, who also
had been unrecognized in youth. A new appreciation for socialism replaces former but now shoddy business ideals, and he
discards the plan for a conventional career in law and politics
with his friend Jim Gogarty.

Suddenly one day he no longer fears his Uncle Al, but with
a new understanding he pities him. This escape from Al's
dominance anticipates Danny's atheism and helps him assert

his independence from his family, despite lasting emotional ties. His atheism brings a sense of confidence and happiness; and, with God destroyed, his old prejudices begin to drop away more easily. He no longer regards the revered University of Chicago as above criticism, and he declares his independence of the economic system by giving up his well-paying service-station job. Finally, he outgrows the nihilism and strong personal attraction of his friend Ed Lanson.

At the end of the pentalogy, Danny cares little what others think. He has cast off many chains, although he is still tied to memories of his past, to romantic notions of himself, and to a rosy ideal of the power of human reason. Man is the new suffering god of his godless universe. Following Theodore Dreiser, Danny pities sorrowful mankind with its confusions and perfidies. But he knows that men, like himself, are able to snatch a purpose in a purposeless world; through promethean endurance and effort, they can create meaning and win a measure of freedom. Danny's new philosophy exists in the tension between despair and confidence.

As Danny leaves for New York, he feels that his break with his past is complete except for his emotion-laden memories; and these he has already begun to purge through writing. The world he is rejecting is brilliantly portrayed by Farrell in the gathering at Mary O'Reilley's wake. Danny thinks his anger against his world has cooled to irony; his hatred is directed not toward the people but toward conditions. His weapon is writing, and his task is to "do battle so that others did not remain unfulfilled as he and his family had been" (*Days*, 401). Beneath his devotion to reason and militance, however, Danny is not very different from the little boy to whom personal affection meant the most, as his grief over Mary O'Flaherty's death shows: "Oh, Mother, oh, Papa, oh, we ungrateful living! This life which he had been so spendthrift of, how precious it was" (*Days*, 393).

Danny is essentially the man of feeling. Life, so short and sad, is important to him now, not as a prelude to heaven or hell, not as a testimony to God's greatness, but as a stage where he may redeem his guilty self by helping to right some of the wrongs with which existence affronts humanity. Danny's protection and guidance of his younger brother Bob are the first concrete examples of his new faith in the power of courageous individual action to change life for the better. He will no longer behave like an acolyte; he now knows his true masters in the world of ideas, and they speak to him of prison-breaking hammers and of the potential dignity of man.

Danny's life naturally lacks the gravitational inevitability we feel in Studs's. Yet Danny's reclamation is entirely plausible, for the series elaborately shows the complex interaction of his character and his environment. In the particulars of his daily living we can feel the origin of his sincere aspirations and his emotional needs that eventually lead to the University of Chicago and to New York City.

As Danny confronts the nebulous future—the world he wants to make—Farrell ends his series with a sure touch. In the call room of the Continental Express Company where Danny had worked, Heinie Mueller, Casey, and Willie Collins romanticize Danny as "a cracker jack clerk" who "knew what the score was" (*Days*, 403). Here is a vivid glimpse of what Danny has renounced, the scene of many past torments. Here is the power of delusion, the sense of people terribly caught in the mechanisms of our civilization, the opposite of what Danny wants. Yet here, too, is the vigorous authority of an established way of life that puts Danny's highfalutin and untested aspirations in a realistic perspective.

II *Method and Meaning*

It is appropriate that Danny should develop more than the other characters, for the keynote of the pentalogy is his struggle for independence. Once his psychology is grasped, the pattern of his behavior is predictable, but his particular acts are not. His growth is neither straight-line nor easygoing, for there is floundering and experimentation. The urgency of his needs drives him *through* experience and gives him a broad knowledge of the city and of people. His needs finally take him from commercial drudgery to the intellectual resources that help him to understand his past and to project his future. Emergence and novelty mark his life, and he exerts partial control over events through intense desire and knowledge.

Danny is, therefore, not cut off from experience as is Studs, who is a prisoner of fixed habits and a barren ideology. Studs's limited awareness dominates in the trilogy, but in the later work

Danny is frequently offstage. Also the family members establish many viewpoints. The resulting autonomy of these convincing people strengthens Danny's characterization, for he grows
through involvement with other persons. Farrell's procedure in
the pentalogy suits the theme of individual growth, just as the
method in *Studs Lonigan* dramatizes the substance of lonely
spiritual impoverishment. Each boy focuses the theme of his
story, and the methods differ accordingly.

Compared to Danny, the adult O'Flahertys and O'Neills—
except for Jim—do not develop radically. In *Father and Son*
the story of the vigorous Jim's deterioration is sustained and
moving. But Tom and Louise O'Flaherty are shadowed by death
from the first. Mary, Lizz, Al, Peg, and Ned enter the story
as mature adults; their values and behavior remain relatively
constant. For instance, Lizz, spouting her incantations and
vilifications, remains a fierce partisan of her family and church,
and Al remains loyal to his ideals of business success and self-
improvement through a study of Lord Chesterfield's letters and
the dictionary. This static quality in Farrell's adults does not,
of course, entirely rule out novelty and growth in their characters. Mary O'Flaherty, in contrast to Jim, becomes increasingly reconciled to the prospect of death. Peg, who fights a
losing battle against her compulsions, comes to dominate her
brothers. Al surrenders some of his authority. These people live.
We believe in their colorful and unique configurations of traits.
We remember them vividly as individuals.

It is recognized that Farrell's repetition of effects in *Studs
Lonigan* powerfully conveys the underlying monotony in his
characters' lives, the wasting passage of time. In the pentalogy
the method of repetition is used more variously. The emphasis
on the family's cultural naïveté heightens our sense of what
Danny must overcome before he finds his way. The frequent
family quarrels and the adults' occasional harshness toward
Danny burn fear and shame into him, thereby making his
ultimate revolt more certain. The reiteration of Al's pretensions
to culture, Ned's New Thought, Peg's resolutions to reform,
Louise's yearnings, Lizz's novenas, and Mary's verbal onslaughts
says a great deal about the deprivation in their lives while it
conveys their stubborn vitality. These people are never bored;
rising above despair, they attack life vigorously. Farrell's repeti-

tion of such traits simultaneously shows the O'Neills' and O'Flahertys' strong will to live and the cultural stunting that affects them as it does Studs and his friends. As first- or second-generation immigrants struggling in a competitive world, they transmit a heritage that is terribly inadequate, but it has the validity of a bludgeoning weapon forged of necessity in the heat of battle.

This stubborn sameness of Farrell's adults over the years creates a special blend of comedy and pathos. Their childlike illusions, such as Al's belief that the true "wise guy" achieves culture through decorum, distorts reality into eccentric patterns. These illusions contrast with Jim's hard-headed views and Danny's intellectualism. Danny learns that an event has many causes, but his family clings hopefully to the simple belief in unitary causation. Especially through Lizz and Mrs. O'Flaherty, Farrell develops a broad and rich humor, a quality of his writing often unrecognized. Like a blowzy witch, Lizz sprinkles holy water or has a mass said to shape the future to her desire. We sympathize with her action, for it naïvely reflects a Christian concept of the power of spirit in the world; and her faith measures the immensity of her need. The illusions that sustain Farrell's adults are profoundly pragmatic, yet ironically they are often handicaps in the struggle for worldly advantage—as when Lizz funnels Jim's earnings into the Church. Because the family's misreading of reality is both comic and pathetic, it has more color and more power to arouse our sympathy than does Danny, who intellectually advances beyond his relatives.

The O'Neills and the O'Flahertys are deeply rooted in their culture: they can escape neither their historical past nor the demanding present. In love and in strife, they act out social process with convincing naïveté; they quarrel, but they stick together and help each other. Their mutual loyalty shows the common need of first- and second-generation Americans for support from family and cultural tradition. Their belligerence derives from the violent past of their ancestors who had fought foreign invaders, but it feeds on harsh economic struggle and on the cultural strife between generations, a conflict intensified by the "greenhorn" background of the adults. The scheming, the shouting, the blows, the talk of splitting skulls with skillets are deeply engrained traits that show them, in effect, meeting their problems with the habits and language developed from their Irish past. They live by social and religious dogma, as seen in their class and racial prejudices: Al's uplift philosophy, and Lizz's novenas. The more illusory or otherworldly their beliefs, the more those beliefs show character as an outgrowth of active historical forces.

Farrell's method spotlights his characters under institutional pressures from family, school, church, job, tavern, and street. We especially feel the power of money in their lives. The children know meatless suppers, and their escapades are often a consequence of deprivation. Peg as hotel cashier, Jim as expressman, Al as salesman, and minor characters like Martha Morton struggle to advance or to hold their own. Each sees his predicament from his worm's-eye view, although Jim also has the perspective of unionism and Al of the success myth. The personalities of these two men, in particular, are shaped by their jobs, a major source of the meaningful contrast between them. Thereby Farrell displays the broad human meaning of twentieth-century capitalism, from its powerful competitive constraint to its genuine opportunities. These books show in detail what it means to have been a big-city, Irish-American Catholic, of modest income, during the first three decades of this century —one reason Farrell is a significant Catholic novelist.

The prolonged affair between Peg and Lorry Robinson, a speculator and a business man, is significant in this connection. It links the major characters to a world they cannot enter: the power struggle between giant economic rivals, and the interlocking of big business and politics. This subplot adds a social dimension to the story, but here, as elsewhere in his narrative, Farrell observes the limits imposed by his characters' degree of awareness. For Peg, Lorry's financial maneuvers signify only a golden dream of possible happiness and a chance to show her personal loyalty; for the families, Lorry is merely the cause of Peg's drunken unhappiness. The affair itself effectively contrasts to the deeper love between Jim and Lizz. By his method, Farrell translates social realities into personal meanings, the stuff of happiness or despair. By and large, he keeps to the objective method developed in *Studs Lonigan:* life is presented as experienced by individuals. But he multiplies the number of his major characters and points of view into a more complex web of experience. The result is a broader, if less powerful, picture of historical realities in personal terms than that given in the story of Studs.

The twenty-five hundred pages of the loosely jointed Danny O'Neill books show little formal plotting, although causal relationships are everywhere; and narrative strands, like the story of Peg and Lorry Robinson, hold some suspense. The episodes are most easily seen as a panorama, as a vast succession of scenes leading to many climaxes and to a fitting conclusion for Danny. It would indeed be difficult to justify formally all the episodes; yet, when the five books are examined as a unit, they reveal a unique structure with its own logic. This structure is appropriate to Danny's position as a son in two families, to the slowly rising curve of his personal development, to the three-generation process which transforms immigrant stock from laborer to intellectual American, and to the large rhythms of life flowing through the books: birth and death, growth and decay, regeneration and sterility. The result is not so intensely dramatic as in *Studs Lonigan*, but it is more inclusive, for here Farrell significantly extends his story of the making of Americans. He broadens the implicit indictment of reigning values and urban conditions, and he presents in Danny the emerging artist—his awakening identity and sources of strength.

CHAPTER 6

The Bernard Carr Trilogy

I Scope and Genesis

Farrell's third major series of novels is the Bernard Carr trilogy: *Bernard Clare* (1946)—after a libel suit by a man of that name, *Clare* was changed to *Carr* in the second novel—*The Road Between* (1949), and *Yet Other Waters* (1952).[1] The trilogy completes the over-all movement in Farrell's three cycles: Studs goes under, Danny discovers his true calling and escapes from Chicago, and after considerable floundering Bernard—a young man distinct from Danny—succeeds as a writer in New York City. The action occurs between 1927 and 1936, overlapping Studs's later years and in effect taking up the thread where Danny dropped it.

When Bernard first comes to New York, the immature young man is penniless and unsure; but his ego is formidable. Like Danny, he is in revolt from his past and wants to write serious fiction. Despite his poverty, he keeps to his ambition and eventually wins recognition as a novelist, and, in the process of struggle and achievement, he finds his identity. The callow rebel of 1927 moves through the difficult years of the Depression—and away from the prescriptions of authoritarian radicals—toward responsible independence in his life and art. The new trilogy continued, therefore, Farrell's story of the American writer nourished by the city. It fulfilled his long-standing ambition to write of New York literary life and of radical political groups.

As late as December, 1941, Farrell considered making Danny the center of his new work. Instead, he decided to drop Danny—who was on the threshold of New York as *My Days of Anger* closed—and to create a new hero modeled upon Patrick McMurtrie, the young Chicagoan in his story "The Only Son." Patrick has elements in common with Danny and Bernard, but

his parents are closer to Mr. and Mrs. Carr than to Jim and Lizz
O'Neill. At this early time Farrell thought of his story as one of
slow but steady corruption: through a series of compromises his
hero, the literary-minded, idealistic middle-class rebel, would
finally succumb not to Stalinism but to the American myth of
success.

In June, 1943, Farrell turned in earnest to his new work,
following a talk with his friend Weldon Kees about the degen-
eration of some literary fellow travelers of the 1930's. Farrell
thought he was able to see objectively the destinies of these
"Stalinist literary men"; and he hoped to convey "the seething
background" of the 1930's, especially through the moral problems and motivation of his hero, whom he partially identified
with two friends from the 1920's in a letter to James Henle,
June 2, 1943.

But the writing came hard; in February, 1944, he made his
fifth start on *Bernard Clare*. He decided to drop the family and
the situation of "The Only Son," as well as some sophisticated
New York characters, and to follow his own early New York
experience more closely. He cut out an affair of Bernard's (later
used in the story "Side Street") and eliminated the characters
Danny O'Neill and Ed Lanson, who had wandered into the
new work. He clarified his plan for the three volumes: (I)
Bernard's youthful failure in New York and his return to Chicago; (II) Bernard's compromise with capitalism, which brings
him outer success but "the thingification of the inner world . . .
as a substitute for inner development" (letter to James Henle,
February 6, 1944); and (III) the resulting deep moral failure,
showing "the ravaging consequences of capitalism" on Bernard's
personality (letter to James Henle, September 9, 1944).

Until Farrell finished *The Road Between* in 1949, his plan,
as he expressed it in a letter to Harry Levin, April 1, 1946,
usually called for Bernard to end "in utter disintegration," with
nowhere to go except the Church. He felt, as he wrote to
Meyer Schapiro, September 11, 1947, that Bernard's "return from
escape" would reveal more about the temper of the times than
would Danny's "opposite pattern of breaking to freedom." A
major problem, he realized, in writing to Calder Willingham
on March 15, 1948, was to create a sense of tragedy: Bernard
must have "sufficient seeds of dependency . . . so that he de-

generates," yet be sympathetically presented as a person of "capacity and intelligence." One feels that Bernard, at the end of *The Road Between,* might go either up or down.

After a period of indecision, Farrell decided in 1949 to end his trilogy on a note of hope and integration. While planning *Yet Other Waters* he began to think of Bernard, as he told Stanley Pargellis in a letter of February 3, 1949, as "going forward and finding a sense of identity with the positive aspects of his background" and with "the possibilities of American life. . . ." He imagined Bernard as an extension of the "psychologically positive" Art McGoorty of the early story "Two Brothers," a person "who is likely to develop and mature" (letter to James Henle, March 13, 1951). Farrell's decision about the direction Bernard would take in *Yet Other Waters* permitted him to write with a greater feeling of integration at a time of personal troubles. But the writing still came hard, for as he expressed it to James Henle on December 11, 1949, "I saw the problem then without the psychology of the problem." His formidable task was to make the notion of human self-fulfillment come alive through the details of his hero's psychology and personal relationships. By October, 1951, Farrell was bringing *Yet Other Waters* to a close, and he was recuperating from an illness at his sister's home in California. More than eight years of laborious writing had gone into Bernard's story.

II *Bernard's Story*

In its final form the Carr trilogy brings together several matters of importance to Farrell. He wrote to Mencken on July 2, 1943, that he wanted to tell what happened, spiritually and artistically, to a generation of New York writers and intellectuals who were either Communists or fellow travelers. (In this respect *The Road Between* and *Yet Other Waters* approximate *romans à clef.*) He felt that their relatively sophisticated story would enrich his picture of contrasting values and milieus in America. Moreover, he intended his hero to mirror the economic and spiritual struggles he had known. From a working-class family, Bernard illustrates Chekhov's statement used as the epigraph to *Bernard Clare*: "What writers belonging to the upper class have received from nature for nothing, plebeians acquire at the cost of their youth." Bernard, Farrell noted in a letter to F. O. Mat-

thiessen of May 12, 1946, is quite unlike James Joyce's Stephen
Dedalus: Bernard comes from a "low level of culture," starts
from scratch against heavy odds, and has to "find everything for
himself." When he gets to New York, Bernard knows he has had
no real youth; for him, the cost of becoming an artist is high.
Moreover, Bernard represents every artist's lonely struggle to
solve "the problem of sincerity" by trying to make his words and
actions express honestly his insights and real feelings. "In this
sense," Farrell wrote to James Henle, October 16, 1944, "sincerity isn't an ideal in itself. It is a prerequisite of getting at . . .
life and one's image of oneself"—an essential element in the
writer's effort to interpret experience.

Eventually Bernard defines himself *vis-à-vis* his boyhood past,
the economic order, his lovers and his wife, and especially the
American Communist party, which tries to use him for its political ends. In his struggle, he must first surmount his laboring-
class origins and then the obstacles—and temptations—represented by middle-class philistinism, domestic life, and radical
communism. He comes to realize that communism, in its way,
parallels the capitalistic culture he resents in *Bernard Clare*.

Each system shows a split between theory and practice, brings
broken promises and frustration, runs over human beings, and
fears creative independence. Thus through Bernard, Farrell returned to familiar themes. Like Henry James, Theodore Dreiser,
Sherwood Anderson, and others before him, he took up the artist's relation to society—a special case of his general interest in
the social making of Americans. Bernard's life, somewhat like
Farrell's and Danny's, becomes a search for integrity, the struggle to be himself through serious writing.

Farrell used the Communist theme to underscore the continuity of his three major cycles. Ironically, the party's authori-
tarianism brings Bernard to himself. In effect, he learns that
Communists are moral cousins to Studs: absolutists whose idealism—or fanatic faith—sanctions their efforts to be strong, tough,
and the "real stuff" in politics and art—or, less kindly, hooligans
with a philosophy. But they pay the price of a shattered integrity and of a withered inner life. A small example may be
seen in Bernard's realization that his friends feel free to sing the

Marseillaise only because the party line toward France had changed. Whereas Farrell's Communists behave on a higher level like Studs, Bernard becomes more and more like a mature version of Danny.

Three crowd scenes of Communist demonstrations taken from the three novels show Bernard's progression. In 1927, on the night Sacco and Vanzetti were executed, the rebellious Bernard, although no Communist, is strong for social justice and as capable of "solidarity" with Communist-manipulated demonstrators as Studs is with his gang. In 1932, he marches with some reservations in the Communist May Day parade. Finally, in 1936, he watches the May Day marchers from the curb; aloof, he sees them as both dupes and deceivers, Stalin's "local boys" (*Yet*, 301), corruptors of the Revolution. He thinks: "He was alone here, as he had been in Chicago in his boyhood" (*Yet*, 404).

But Bernard's isolation is that of integrity and not that arising from aggressive hostility toward others, as in Studs, or from rejection by others, as in Danny. Like Danny, Bernard is a stranger in a world he never made and has a tough endurance Studs never really had; but he has outgrown Danny's frustration and rage. Instead of feeling Danny's early insecurity, he knows he can "walk the streets with confidence" (*Yet*, 414). Like Farrell, he becomes more aware of the evil flowing straight out of men's hearts and minds, as distinct from the evil of social injustice. In *Judgment Day,* the Communist parade held hope for the deceived, the "prisoners of starvation" (*Yet*, 404) like the Lonigans; but, in *Yet Other Waters,* the Communist marchers are themselves prisoners of the deceit they practice.

As in the Danny O'Neill series, the central story is the hero's growth. At twenty-one, Bernard is a confused romantic who spends half of 1927 in New York City trying to write. He believes most people live frustrated lives filled with the "dulled sadness" (*Clare*, 106) that is also felt by the main character in his story "Someday." His view of existence as a drab affair and as a race with Time in which Death is the ultimate winner masks his angry determination to expose through his writing life's shame and injustice. His immaturity is seen in his chip-on-shoulder attitude, his rigid emotional sets, and his tendency to think in clichés and code words. In these respects, he is like Studs.

But Bernard's identification with Sacco and Vanzetti stiffens his backbone as one of the "unforgetting ones" (*Clare*, 51), and the enormity of the injustice he believes they suffered places his personal problems in a more reasonable perspective. His jobs selling cigars and advertising sharpen his sense of human variety and help him to understand the plight of misfits in a society all out for money and progress. He becomes more aware of life's complexity and its accidental quality, especially evident in the mysterious "crossings" of human destinies (*Clare*, 202). He learns much about the range of good and evil in men. He develops compassion, regarding humanity as mired in fleshly desires and ignorance but always reaching for the sun. His love affair with Eva Stone, a young married woman, helps restore his badly shaken ego and enables him to define his aims with greater certainty.

Although Bernard publishes nothing during his first stay in New York, he progresses toward his goal of writing significant fiction. He dimly sees that he must discard the "code words" of his memory and find the right words to faithfully objectify his feelings (*Clare*, 107). He arrives at some working principles, such as the advantage of combining "very tender" insights and "a savage indictment" in his writing (*Clare*, 316). He begins to see himself more clearly; for example, he understands the personal vanity and the guilt in his affair with Eva. As *Bernard Clare* ends, he is still relatively immature, still groping, a parochial Nietzschean who can be disagreeably self-assertive. But at the core of his personality is a strong will to fight tenaciously for what he wants. He at least knows that he is a "collection of somebodies wanting to be a synthesis of somebodies" through his art (*Clare*, 160).

The Road Between opens more than four years later in March, 1932. Bernard and his bride Elizabeth are living in a New York basement apartment. Bernard's first novel, *The Father,* a book about his boyhood neighborhood, brings him recognition but little else; yet, with a baby coming, he gives up a job to work on his second novel, *Unshapely Things,* a story suggested by the married life of Eva Stone and her husband. Bernard still feels a Zarathustrian defiance and loneliness, but his art permits him to harness much of his inner torment. Emerging from the 1920's into the 1930's, he is well along on the road between his conventional Chicago past—reflected in chapters about his and Elizabeth's families—and his radically different New York life. With increasing confidence, he stands between these two worlds —each in its way hostile to the artist's effort to find his own truth. Bernard's growing understanding of each is the measure of his development in this novel.

He comes to understand his crude father's sexual and cultural frustrations. He sees that his pious Catholic mother dreads unimportance as much as he does and that she seeks immortality not through art but through religion. He realizes that, to the faithful, the Catholic Church he has rejected clothes life with meaning and dignity—as he tries to do in his writing. Also he begins to see the disparity between Communist theory and practice—the aggression clothed in befogging formulas—an insight that will lead him to reject communism as he rejected the church, in order to keep faith with the realities of his experience. The road between that he travels thus leads from mind to heart. Eventually, the journey will enable him to heal a split in his consciousness between the rational and the emotional. His earlier condemnation of his past and his acceptance of Marxism were steps toward freedom, but his heart now feels the tug of loyalty to family and to native traditions as part of the truth he will affirm in his writing. *The Road Between* ends in 1933: Bernard publishes *Unshapely Things*, he wins a Loewenthal Fellowship, and Elizabeth's baby is born dead.

Yet Other Waters traces Bernard's life for a year and a half beginning in the spring of 1935; and, as before, interspersed Chicago scenes take us back to his origins. The Carrs, now fairly well off, live in a comfortable New York apartment on West Ninth Street with their baby son Philip. Bernard's reputation is established: he has sold *Unshapely Things* to Hollywood and has written a book of short stories and a new novel, *Paddy Stanton*. He has begun his fourth novel, *A Boy's World*, which he describes as "a kind of emotional adventure in the exploration of my own past" (*Yet*, 78). Early in *Yet Other Waters* he pickets in a department-store strike directed by the party, just as Farrell took part in the 1935 Ohrbach strike. With other pickets, he is briefly jailed; and his revulsion at this physical constraint foreshadows his struggle for complete artistic freedom. The scornful Communist playwright Paul Drummond wants

writers to propagandize for social justice. To him, freedom is
merely "a fine big word," "a petit-bourgeois illusion" (*Yet*, 96);
but Bernard knows that, if his talent is to flourish, no one can
tell him what is in his head and what he should write. His
speech at the 1935 American Writers Congress emphasizes the
cultural need for artistic freedom and diversity. The congress
enables him to see Communist intrigue from the inside; and it
teaches him that, if the fight for justice is conducted on Communist terms, it does not lead to a better culture. Resisting in-
ducements to make his writing follow the party line, he explains
that he seeks "to rediscover and put down . . . some of my own
continuity" (*Yet,* 79).

Bernard seeks to rediscover his Chicago past in order to
understand himself. That past is alive in his family and Elizabeth's. His brothers and sisters are still trapped in the working
conditions and limited culture that he so bitterly resented in
his youth. His mother, a fervent Catholic, is a dying old woman
living with the memory of her loveless marriage and preoccupied
with dark thoughts of sin and death. His father-in-law Mr.
Whelan, a successful undertaker, clings to conventional respectability; but he is a man of some force and dignity. Although
Bernard rejects many of his family's values, he increasingly understands his people and respects their individuality.

Maturity of this order contributes to Bernard's eventual
public denunciation of the party for its tactics of violence and
deceit, which Bernard observed at close range when Communist
trouble-makers disrupted a peaceful Socialist meeting and then
denied all responsibility. Bernard takes his action about the time
his son Philip takes his first faltering steps. His renewed love
for Elizabeth similarly signifies the distinctive human thing that
the Communists deny, just as earlier in the novel Elizabeth's
face—"soft, round, absorbed, and beautiful as she gazed down
at the baby who was noisily and greedily sucking at the bottle"
(*Yet,* 109-10)—contrasts to the remote, unreal quality of the
Communist-dominated Writers Congress. In effect, Bernard
ranges himself on the side of loyalty and love in human
relationships—in agreement with Farrell's conviction, as expressed in his letter to Bruno Bettelheim of March 20, 1948,
that a faith in ideas and in the creative imagination "demands
an emphasis of love in the human personality, rather than of

hate." As the trilogy ends, Bernard's mother dies, and Elizabeth is expecting another child.

III *Theme and Accomplishment*

The third volume makes clear that the trilogy, like much of Farrell's work, establishes an opposition between forces of life and death in modern America and shows the growth of life out of death. Bernard believes that death is life's framework and end (the extinction of awareness) and that whatever diminishes awareness, whether because of rigid attitudes or cultural sterility, is a form of death-in-life. It may be said, then, that absolutisms like the Catholic Church and the party, although meeting deep human needs, are blinders to help fearful men cope with the fact of death. Bernard regards his writing as an opposite method of outwitting death: a splurge of consciousness, a sustained effort to intensify awareness and understanding. He learns that to write with truth he must constantly return to the flux of experience—to *his* feelings and thoughts.

He observes, for example, that Communist generalizations about the bourgeoisie do not capture the reality of individual New Yorkers. The fumbling of his baby son Philip with a set of blocks brings him back to the important truth that the test of theory is in experience. He realizes, with humility, that he generalizes about man's cultural development over the centuries without knowing "a hell of a lot about a baby—my own baby, to be specific" (*Yet*, 335). Such personal experiences are the basis for Bernard's growing distrust of all formal systems claiming perfection and finality; "for other and yet other waters are ever flowing on" (Farrell's quotation from Heraclitus in a letter to James Henle, October 31, 1949).

This Heraclitean, pragmatic theme is restated through a parallel set of symbols: the women in Bernard's life. The haunting vision of Elsie Cavanagh, the girl he adored as a young boy, is an ideal of perfection like the Catholic Church; and Alice is his seductive Communist mistress who would like him to knuckle under. Elizabeth, one of Farrell's best women characters, is intuitive, warm, sensible, and loyal to Bernard and to the needs of her family—a good example of feminine "realism" in contrast to masculine "idealism." Bernard's renewed affection for her is a return to a love which, like a heightened conscious-

ness, is a creative breach of death's power and one that gives
added point to Bernard's—and Danny's—earlier angers and hates.

Bernard grows through his ability to perceive and reject the
disembodied ideal, the seductive Absolute, in his emotional life
and in his thinking. His final wisdom is to seek the attainable
ideal in the ever changing present reality and not to locate it in
a fantasy of the past or future, as Studs does, or in a utopia
of this world or a heaven of the next. It is the wisdom, strangely
echoing Hawthorne, of Saint-Just's phrase, "Happiness is a new
idea" (*Road*, 66). For Bernard, this saying summarizes a way of
life embracing a democratic social philosophy, a pragmatic trust
in experience, a naturalistic metaphysics, and an ethics of self-
fulfillment in one's personal and occupational lives.

Judged as fiction, the Carr trilogy is weaker than the two
earlier series—unfortunately so, for its climactic position calls for
strength. At the heart of the difficulty lies Farrell's uncertain
conception of Bernard's character and fate. The original intention to have Bernard return to Mother Church or to Stalinism—
as some of the characters in Bernard's fiction do—did not square
with Farrell's compelling need to have Bernard become tri-
umphantly self-sustaining. The emotional drive and the intellectual conception did not always coincide in this series, and characterization suffered as a result. The discontinuity between Bernard of the first book and Bernard of the later volumes is dis-
turbing. The cloudiness in his character cannot be entirely ac-
counted for by Farrell's effort to highlight the problem of
identity or to avoid the "gianticism" of "Wolfeism"—the emotionally inflated and monotonous patterning of events as experienced by the exceptional young man who feels superior to
others (letter to F. O. Matthiessen, May 12, 1946). Farrell's lack
of detachment toward Bernard shows in his inability to establish
and keep a clarifying point of view.

Nor do the Bernard Carr books flow from the almost instinc-
tive knowledge of place and manners that is evident in Farrell's
Chicago novels. Studs is rooted in his narrow environment, a
natural carrier of its values; and Danny knows his world thoroughly. But Bernard does not really know his world; he is
homeless in a way Studs and Danny never are. Although this
quality is not inappropriate to a seeker, Farrell's method, as
Blanche Gelfant has shown, fails to convey the density of Ber-

nard's inner life—that very flux he learned to trust. His constant self-questioning, so conscious and routine, lacks a sense of urgency. It inadequately reflects his emotional turbulence and the substance of his thought. For a fertile writer, he is too seldom portrayed as in creative interplay with ideas, and too often, perhaps, as in merely hostile relationship to his environment—as a would-be destroyer whose theory of the use of literature approximates the Communist dictum that art is a weapon.

Farrell justified his plebeian hero's character in explaining to Henle in a letter of May 28, 1946, that he had tried to place Bernard "on the same plane as the other characters"; he did not want to have "culture . . . conceal reality in the books." The intention is praiseworthy, yet we miss a compelling sense in Bernard that human culture, in its broadest sense, *is* his reality, his very livelihood as a writer. He once mentions to Elizabeth that he constantly talks about the crisis in civilization, the rise of socialism, and human culture—but neither he nor any other character creates the sense that social abstractions are convulsively alive within them. The autonomous "social universe," the seething background Farrell wished to catch, is clouded over by Bernard's narrow self-absorption.

Conversely, the odyssey of Bernard's soul, a journey that claims Farrell's ultimate interest, is often weakly projected through external events, with the result that we feel impoverishment and dissociation within the action. And Bernard's character is inadequately sustained by the world he inhabits. To be sure, the Chicago scenes, some of the Chicago characters—notably Elizabeth's father Mr. Whelan and Mrs. Carr—and a number of objective New York sequences show much of Farrell's earlier power. Some of the Communists, especially Jake, Sam, and Sophie, come alive at intervals; but, by and large, the New York writers, publishers, and radicals are ghostly figures who, moreover, inadequately convey those social realities of magnitude that Bernard confronts. Although Farrell's hero succeeds in his significant quest, the world he moves in lacks the solidity and meaningful implication of that other rejected world in *Studs Lonigan,* and Bernard himself insufficiently represents the positive ideal made real. Farrell's objective method is less resourceful and successful here than in his series on Studs and Danny.

Nevertheless, with a brilliance of conception, Farrell rounds
out with the trilogy the organic story begun in *Young Lonigan;*
for Bernard's hard-won wisdom and freedom are ultimately a
triumph over the spiritual rigidity seen in rudimentary form in
Studs. In Farrell's writing, Danny makes the first stand for the
creative life; but it is Bernard who wrests that life from impoverished origins. He nourishes it in a conventional world that
gives pre-eminence to middle-class respectability and commercial success. He protects it from cynical radicalism. Bernard's
protean enemy, in its effort to tyrannize over the creative spirit,
will try to stultify, seduce, and coerce. To meet the variable
challenge, Bernard, in his rise, necessarily must function on
more social levels than Danny. The trilogy is thus unusually
ambitious, if only partly successful, in its concern with the artist's
full entanglement with society. Unquestionably the Bernard Carr
novels extend and enrich Farrell's picture of America.

CHAPTER 7

The Individual Novels and the Tales

In addition to the major works—*Studs Lonigan,* the O'Neill-O'Flaherty pentalogy, the Bernard Carr trilogy, and *A Universe of Time*—Farrell has published five other novels and well over two hundred short stories. These tales and individual novels round out and complicate his fictional world; for, as we have often indicated, they interlace with his multivolume works in settings, characters, and themes. The story "Shorty Leach" from *Sound of a City* (1962) illustrates the relationship. This tale brings us back to the Washington Park-Chicago Loop axis; and the narrator is Danny O'Neill, a man in his late forties, whose memories of his boyhood friend Shorty reveal his own maturity and his intense attachment to his personal past, as well as details of his early life.

Danny tells of two conversations twenty-five years apart that he had with Shorty, a character from the tale "A Practical Joke" and *The Young Manhood of Studs Lonigan,* where he sings the blues at the famous New Year's Eve party. Initially, the tale returns us to August, 1925, when Danny is in his first quarter at the university and when Shorty anticipates a happy future. It skips briefly back to a time before Danny moved to the Fifty-eighth Street neighborhood in 1917 and when he knew Shorty's reputation as a fine athlete. Then it moves ahead to Danny's last meeting in 1950 with the beaten Shorty. By giving the essentials of Shorty's unsuccessful life over a period of thirty-five years, the tale traces one more American destiny in the populous society of Farrell's world. It also displays Shorty's relationships to familiar characters from earlier books: Phil Rolfe, Jack Morgan, Marty Mulligan, Milt Rosenplatz, and Sonny Green. Shorty, like so many of his contemporaries, is firmly fixed in his time and place. Similarly, most of the other tales and the individual novels add depth and detail to Farrell's picture.

I   Gas-House McGinty

During the fall of 1931, while in Paris, Farrell wrote *Gas-House McGinty* (1933), his second novel. This work directly influenced *The Young Manhood of Studs Lonigan* and *Judgment Day*—for example, Farrell wrote its dream chapter in preparation for the death fantasies of Studs. As recently as the preceding July, Farrell had sent the prospectus of his new book to James Henle, who promised him an advance when his manuscript was under way. By September 13, Farrell had completed 329 pages; and Henle's immediate response of September 28, 1931, was favorable: "I like them, I like your method of work and I like everything about you." Henle sent an advance of two hundred dollars and issued the contract. With this encouragement, Farrell worked at top speed, and, by October 7, he had completed most of the first draft. He made final revisions in February, 1933, while in New York City.

Gas-House McGinty had simmered in Farrell's mind since 1927 when he submitted a story "Harry and Barney" (the original versions of McGinty and Willie Collins) to Professor Linn. In 1931, he designed his novel as the first part of a trilogy on the Amalgamated Express Company in Chicago, for which Farrell, his father, and two of his brothers had worked. The action of the three books was to revolve around the Wagon Call Department under the successive direction of four chief dispatchers. Much of the manuscript for the unpublished second and third volumes was destroyed by the 1946 fire in Farrell's New York apartment; but revisions of unburnt portions may be seen in about a dozen of Farrell's Chicago tales, including the four about Willie Collins, who was to have been the central character of the final book.

Farrell linked the expressmen of his trilogy to the more prosperous middle-class circles in which the Lonigans moved, and he made the sixteen-year-old Danny O'Neill and his father, the stricken Jim, important characters in *Gas-House McGinty*. There we read Jim's prayer for his children: "God, I know the game, and it's beat me. Please don't let it beat them! Please God! God, make them sluggers, make them slug, and take it, and slug again."[1] We see Danny's growing feeling of being a nobody as he flounders in a nether commercial world that is poles apart from the enlightenment he later found at the University of Chicago.

Farrell originally called his new work "The Madhouse" and described it as "a Romance of Commerce and Service." In the undated prospectus sent to Henle, he stated: "it cannot be written as a straight novel, but must have its own structure worked out; and I do not favor having that a simple series of stories, as, say, Seaver did in his 'The Company.' Rather it should be something in which the characters are massed, and in which the sense of the composite picture is more developed, so that one gets a sense of them squirming inside this large institution."[2] He wrote in a letter to Henle, dated September 13, 1931, that plot and movement could be "developed by allowing the incidental jokes, quarrels, jealousies, promotions, deaths, and felt-pressures of the external environment (economic depression) to lead from scene to scene." Somewhat later, before he reworked the first draft, he decided—as he told Henle on January 8, 1932—to make McGinty the dominant character in order to "give an added coherence to the book" beyond that gained by "a style, a common scenery, and . . . a loose connection of the characters' work."

The completed novel focuses on the hectic Wagon Call Department during the summer of 1920, and the slight narrative follows the fortunes of frustrated Chief Dispatcher Ambrose J. McGinty, a proud man whose eventual demotion to route inspector parallels the "fall" of the hero in the song "Down Went McGinty." But, in a real sense, the office itself remains the protagonist. The anonymous, blaring telephone conversations of the call clerks and the incessant sadistic banter create a nightmarish collective personality; and all the office workers from the lowliest to the supervisor merge into one commercial function. Paradoxically, the irritations of the job intensify a crude individualism within the hierarchy of authority. In the give and take of the Call Department, the men release their hostilities through aggressive speech and practical jokes. They unguardedly reveal some deep concerns of their personal lives, and they reflect current events in their talk and inner consciousness. As Farrell accurately wrote to Henle on September 13, 1931, his characters "bring everything down to the Call Department,

and, so to speak, dump it." The crowded, claustrophobic office
thus remains the central stage, one rich in social implication.
Otherwise, Farrell tellingly indicates the social context through
scenes of McGinty and other office workers at home or on the
street and through interchapters about the wagon men. Only
rarely do company executives of the upper managerial level,
men remote and feared like gods, step into the action.

McGinty is a small triumph of characterization. This vain,
restless fat man can be petty and cruel; but his vulnerability
and his clumsy, naïve search for satisfaction in love and work
arouse our sympathy. His existence affords him no dignity and
little opportunity for affection, yet he is his own worst enemy.
He longs for power, but he can neither master his wife nor
command the respect of others. Only in his troubled, erotic
dreams can he triumph, and even in them his guilts and appre-
hensions drag him down. The individuality of other expressmen,
like Heinie Mueller, Casey, and Francis McGillicuddy, emerges
from the welter of office talk and business.

Farrell may have overworked the dialogue for purposes of
narration and characterization (he cut the Vanguard text for
the Avon reprint edition), yet the men's frantic talk, functioning
as release from devitalizing routine, makes its point and shows
Farrell's ability to handle a robust vernacular:

HELLO WAGON . . . '
By the way, Heinie, how's the wife? Cole asked.
The Dutchman's wife is takin' in washin' from the Jiggs out on the
south side, yelled Mac.
Heinie looked at McGinty. The department grew tense.
None of that goes with me, McGinty. Cut it out! Heinie said.
I was only kiddin', Mac said.
I don't like your kiddin', Heinie said.
Mac turned and answered a phone.
If these other guys in the depots want to take that from you they
can. I won't, said Heinie.
Several route inspectors smiled at Mac's discomfort.
Jesus, Heinie, I'm sorry. I didn't mean nothin', Mac said.
Well, try another way of kiddin' the next time, Heinie said.
HELLO WAGON . . .
The wife's two months gone, Heinie said to Cole (*McGinty*, 135).

Despite the dreary human material with which the novel deals, it remains a fresh, meaningful treatment of an area rarely explored. It vividly dramatizes the shaping—and scarring—of character through occupation and thus complements the stories of Studs and Danny, which constantly return to the effect of leisure activity and family relationships upon personal growth. It vigorously re-creates the human significance of the commercial purgatory Danny fled.

II   This Man and This Woman

This Man and This Woman (1951), a successful minor novel, returns to the milieu of the Express Company a quarter of a century later in relating the domestic catastrophe of the aging couple Walt and Peg Callahan. Walt is sixty-three, ten years older than Peg. He is a respected and capable terminal dispatcher who has worked his way up from the wagons. A veteran of almost fifty years with the company, he is one of the few survivors of the old free-wheeling days of Gas-House McGinty, Jim O'Neill, and Porky Mulroy. A kind, likable man, his great desire is to live out his years happily and actively with his wife and grandchildren, enjoying the comforts of life he feels he has earned. Instead, he is stabbed to death by Peg, herself a victim of advanced paranoiac delusions, of voices saying "He'll kill you."

This short novel thus becomes a concentrated study in paranoia. Its theme, as Farrell noted in a letter to Henle on May 11, 1954, is a variation on the idea of "biological tragedy," earlier developed in the stories of Jim O'Neill, Tom O'Flaherty, and Bernard's parents, as well as in Farrell's unpublished novel *Invisible Swords*. The erosion of human life through physical and psychological causes is seen here particularly in Peg's aberration. The action is limited to the last six days in Walt's life, and it builds upon Peg's growing paranoia that suffocates her former buoyant spirit. The novel roots Peg's illness in her childhood and conveys her sense of the loss of all that made her life as a young woman desirable. It convincingly depicts the critical transition from an extreme form of irrational nagging to murderous action. Farrell achieves his effect by switching back and forth between the viewpoints of Peg and Walt, the two major characters.

Farrell sees his aging couple, once so much in love, with an unsentimental detachment and an implicit sympathy. He does not skim over the dreary and often ugly details of their daily relationship; he invokes no easy, soothing explanation of the monstrous torment in Peg; and he shows Walt in all his stolid, well-meaning obtuseness. He thoroughly understands the Callahans. Perhaps the novel's greatest strength lies in the convincing and sympathetic portrayal of Peg's change into the very thing she thinks she sees in the likable Walt. Appropriately minimizing the social background, Farrell in this bare and unadorned story explores seemingly unbridgeable differences between man and wife—between the masculine and the feminine—with an intensity suitable to Peg's obsessional character.

III   Ellen Rogers

Ellen Rogers (1941), also a story of blighted love in Chicago, concerns an affair in 1925 between twenty-one-year-old Edmond Lanson and Ellen, two years his junior and just out of high school. The novel is Farrell's first sustained study of a woman, and he adds in Ed Lanson an original character to his gallery of men. Farrell, who began serious work on his story in December, 1940, felt the need of a vacation from writing about the O'Neills and the O'Flahertys. At first he intended no more than a novelette centering on Ellen, conceived as a shallow flapper not unlike the character Eloise in his story "Seventeen." But before long his imagination fastened upon Ed Lanson, who is modeled after a close friend of Farrell's from the 1920's. Early in March, as Farrell revealed to John Dewey, he was rereading Nietzsche as background study for Ed's character. The work developed rapidly into a chronicle whose events are tied together by Ellen's growing passion for Ed, and whose mounting climax, as Mencken wrote to Farrell in September, 1941, is managed with impressive effect. By the middle of 1941, Farrell had completed the writing except for a few revisions.

Compared to his earlier novels, *Ellen Rogers* depends only slightly upon minor characters and upon dense social background, partly because Farrell had begun his work as a novelette. But, when his book became the history of an affair, Farrell continued to play down the social context and the supporting cast of characters; he felt he should concentrate on his lovers' personal relationships. He also believed that his earlier books adequately gave the essential middle-class background for Ellen and Ed. Here, then, was an opportunity to carry out his plan of gradually expanding his "social universe" from its carefully laid base. He would still keep to Chicago; but he could proceed, as he explained in a letter to C. A. Pearce of May 8, 1941, to unfold new characters "from the background that I have tried firmly to establish in the books I've already written." The story thus lacks the massive social impact of *Studs Lonigan,* where we see Studs in a full context and where we observe his habits, shared by many friends, as they are being formed. The origins of Ed's destructive egotism are left in obscurity, and he is presented as a loner, unique in his revolt against established values.

The narrow focus of the novel is suggested by Thomas Mann's judgment, expressed in a letter to Farrell of September 26, 1941, that *Ellen Rogers* "is one of the best love-stories I know, of unusual truthfulness and simplicity." Mann believed that Ellen's agony and humiliation following her abandonment by Ed were brilliantly portrayed. She is, indeed, Farrell's far lesser Anna Karenina, the female in the grip of passion. Once she is in love, her calculating worldliness and her self-sufficiency disappear. Her superficial life assumes increased meaning as depths of devotion and suffering develop. In a sequence of effective episodes, we see her growing helplessness before Ed, but her floundering efforts to win him back lead only to fury and desperation. Then Farrell presents her final abasement and her sense of numb emptiness before she takes her life. One thinks, almost inevitably, of Theodore Dreiser's portrayal in *Sister Carrie* of Hurstwood's dissociation from life and his suicide. The two actions appropriately differ in the characters' psychology and in the pace of the decline; moreover, Dreiser employs no "villain" comparable to Ed. Of the two stories Dreiser's is the more fateful and reveals greater depths of suffering humanity, but Farrell's accomplishment is nevertheless memorable and affecting.

Although Ellen is the source of emotional strength in this novel, her destroyer, Ed Lanson, interests us more as an individual and as a symbolic figure of the 1920's. Farrell imagined him as a mixture of a middle-class Sanine, a shallow Raskolnikov, and an eighteenth-century rogue transplanted to the 1920's. In short, as Farrell indicated in his letter to C. A. Pearce of April

25, 1941, Lanson is a vulgarized product of "the Ben Hecht, Bodenheim, Cabell, Nietzsche influence." Ed, a character of calculated ambiguity, is not merely morally starved or conventional; he directs his charm, his courage, and his intelligence toward wicked ends. He is a rebel in the cause of Romantic individualism, a kind of debased version of Max Stirner's egotist, a would-be superman. Lanson "uses" others, for whom he shows utter contempt; and he rationalizes his actions through his misconception of Nietzsche's philosophy. He is more dangerous than Studs because he is aware—an accomplished technician in evil.

Like Studs, Ed Lanson is a foil to Danny (significantly *Ellen Rogers* came just before *My Days of Anger*), for essentially he is uncreative and he grows toward irresponsibility and ill will. He takes a road more deathlike than Studs's; he is incapable of true love even in dream. *Ellen Rogers* is remarkable as a love story and as a study of the deceitful heart that awakens love for the pleasure of strangling it. As Hortense Farrell noted when she read the manuscript, it catches much of the spirit of the 1920's in its portrayal of youth's careless squandering of human emotions, even the throwing away of human lives.[3] The theme of waste is evident in *Ellen Rogers* as in *Studs Lonigan*.

IV Boarding House Blues

Ed Lanson and Danny O'Neill are key figures in *Boarding House Blues* (1961), Farrell's sixteenth novel. This uneven but haunting work is the story of a Bohemian colony on Chicago's Near North Side early in 1930. It was mostly written between June and September, 1953, when Farrell was traveling in Spain and France. The novel partly grew out of the author's longstanding interest in a friend's mother, an elderly woman who became the inspiration for the character Bridget O'Dair. Farrell described her to Henle in 1941 as a woman who collected insurance money on two houses she burned down and who took a young lover after her children were grown.

The novel also grew from Farrell's desire to explore the moral lower depths of Bohemia in relation to Danny's growth. In *My Days of Anger* Danny and Ed Lanson sometimes visit the Near North Side; but, as that book closes, they are about to leave in the summer of 1927 for New York City. In *Boarding House*

Blues, although still friendly, they have grown apart. Ed is now married and living in New York City. He shows himself to be as unprincipled as ever on a visit to his Chicago friends, but he is increasingly ineffectual in carrying through his schemes. Danny, who returned from New York early in 1928, is deep in an affair with Anna Brown (Elizabeth, in the Bernard novels), who has a miscarriage. He is trying to get his career started by writing "about the 58th Street boys in the old neighborhood" (*BHB,* 217). Although he has not yet published, he has found his subject matter and knows where he is headed. Regarded as one incarnation of Farrell's composite writer-hero, he is in transition, as it were, between Bernard floundering in *Bernard Clare* and Bernard successful in *The Road Between.*

The surface plot of *Boarding House Blues* is the tawdry conflict between Ed and Bridget O'Dair, the nymphomaniac grandmother, over disputed rights in a disintegrating rooming house for Bohemians on North Michigan Avenue. This conflict calls forth a great expense of energy for trivial ends, and it is set against a background of the irresponsible, sterile lives of the several roomers. Ed busies himself with petty intrigues because he is aimless; like Studs, he is bored with his wasted life and needs to kill time. When we last see Ed, he shows symptoms of a brain tumor that eventually will destroy him. Danny, in contrast, finds time of supreme worth. Like Sherwood Anderson's George Willard of Winesburg, Ohio, he senses the despair in life and knows that its framework is death; but his particular life "wasn't senseless because he had a purpose that would give him the means to find himself on earth" (*BHB,* 152).

Danny's philosophy calls, therefore, for a serious commitment to experience at the price of total risk: "You can swim out, out and out, against the waves and storms of troubles, seeing the unreachable horizon and allowing the illusion to remain that you will reach it, a smooth and calm expanse of waters without waves and storms; or else you can play around the shore, and never know the cold and angry waters of the depths" (*BHB,* 210). The theme of the novel is man's use of his brief lifetime—Farrell's old concern with growth and deterioration, the mysterious alternatives and rhythms of human life. As Danny writes in his notebook: "The question is which 'to be' before we are 'not to be.' There are no Hamlets today who are of Hamlet's quality" (*BHB*, 209). Danny, who chooses "to swim out," passes judgment on all those—Bohemians included—who choose an ignominious and trivial "to be" as they safely play around the shore.

V   New Year's Eve/1929

Closely connected with *Boarding House Blues* and, like it, written in 1953, Farrell's *New Year's Eve/1929* (1967), a short novel, places Danny and his girl Anna once again in Bohemian circles, this time near the University of Chicago campus on the eve of the 1930's, a few months before the time of action in *Boarding House Blues*. They go to a New Year's Eve party given by the third-floor tenants of an apartment building jokingly known as Schmolsky's Culture Center and located on Harper Avenue, a few doors north of Fifty-seventh Street. (In 1929 Farrell sometimes visited friends in the building, called the Coudich Culture Center after its French owner who wanted to make it an artists' colony.) Danny no longer is enrolled at the university; but, as Farrell once did, he uses the Harper Library for study and writing. Much in love with Anna and without a regular job, he thinks of himself as "fighting, day by day, to dedicate himself to his writing."[4]

To the party at Schmolsky's come university students—some, like Pete the Greek and Nathan Lewisberg, are active elsewhere in Farrell's fiction—painters and intellectuals from the Fifty-seventh Street artists' group, and assorted hangers-on who find glamor or excitement in South Side Bohemia. One of these is Beatrice Burns, the only character whom Farrell explores in some depth in the novel. Beatrice is an ex-nurse who knows that she is dying of tuberculosis. Like Tamara in *My Days of Anger*, she cherishes and displays the X-rays of her "rotting" lungs (*NYE*, 13). Haunted by the thought of death, she romanticizes herself as "gay and game" with every guilty cigarette she smokes (*NYE*, 141). In her morbid self-concern, she sees the New Year's Eve celebration primarily as "Bea Burns' death party" (*NYE*, 12), but for most other persons Bea hardly exists. She is unattractive and graceless; and, as Danny understands, she is tritely and "offensively stupid" (*NYE*, 97). She finds a source of vitality, a reason for living, only in gossip and meddling. Danny realizes that the unhappy girl "wanted to know everything she could about other people and their personal lives" in order to fill her own emptiness (*NYE*, 81). Farrell's chief triumph in his novelette is to portray this banal busybody with merciless clarity; and yet, as she clings to a distasteful existence, he awakens his readers' sympathy for her as "a frightened little girl" who still "wanted to . . . dream when there was no use in dreaming" (*NYE*, 144).

It is fitting that Danny should understand Bea. Like her, but in a less personal way, he is keenly aware of coming destruction; and he too dreams when there seems to be little use in it. As Danny explains to Nathan Lewisberg, "I'm racing against time to live and work as best I can before the war comes because when it does, it will be Armageddon" (*NYE*, 61). He believes America, England, and France will line up against Germany and Italy, but is unsure of Russia's allegiance. In Danny's somber vision the New Year's Eve revelers were tragic little people "all marching to unknown destinies . . . in the face of a grim and uncertain world" (*NYE*, 82). Thus, while Bea turns to the trivia of personal intrigue and sentimental thoughts of the past, Danny, equally haunted, looks to the future and to his writing. Once again he is isolated from those like Bea or Studs or Ed Lanson whose sterile values are capped by an early death. *New Year's Eve/1929* glances obliquely at a significant stage in Danny's career. On the threshold of a decade that will bring him hard-won triumphs, the ex-student resolutely pursues his proper work.

VI *The Short Stories*

Years before Farrell conceived *Studs Lonigan,* he had been writing short stories, beginning with the juvenilia published in his high school magazine, *Oriflamme.* At the University of Chicago he continued to write stories. "The Open Road" and "Mary O'Reilley" were composed in 1928; and James Weber Linn's praise in 1929 of "Calico Shoes" in manuscript triggered renewed efforts at story writing that soon led to publication (conversation with Farrell, September 8, 1963). Every year since then Farrell has written many stories. Typically, he keeps them by him for a few years, and sometimes much longer, a practice usually permitting several revisions and explaining the presence of early writings in even his most recent collections, *Side Street and Other Stories* (1961), *Sound of a City* (1962), and *Childhood Is*

Not Forever (1969). To date, he has published approximately
two hundred and twenty-five tales, most of them collected in
thirteen volumes beginning with *Calico Shoes and Other Stories*
(1934), an impressive group of sixteen Chicago pieces that he
first wanted to bring together as *These Chicagoans*. In addition,
he has published two omnibus collections, several paperback
editions of selected stories, and a limited edition of *A Misunder-
standing* (1949). A good many other tales are still uncollected
or in manuscript.

Farrell's tales are additional evidence of his intention to shake
reality like a sack until it is empty. A few of them, as Robert
Morss Lovett said, literally are chips off the blocks of his
novels: early versions or preliminary experiments ("Studs," "Jim
O'Neill"), deletions ("Boys and Girls"), or parts of abandoned
works ("The Hyland Family," "Pat McGee"). The great ma-
jority were written as independent pieces, yet many of these
mesh with the novels and among themselves, thereby helping to
complete the design of Farrell's fiction. All the stories remain
faithful to his version of reality while reflecting his continuing
experience. Thus, they reinforce our impression of his writing
as a loosely organized, expanding work-in-progress.

In this connection, Farrell's use of Danny or his near equivalent in the tales is especially revealing. This autobiographical
character may appear as a small boy mourning his dog Lib or
as a grown man touring Italy in the mid-1950's. Altogether, he
appears in over fifty stories. In a liberal handful of these, tales
like "Boyhood" or "Kilroy Was Here," Danny is himself the
central character. In about ten others the major character who
in all essentials is Danny is unnamed or differently named: for
example, "Autumn Afternoon," "Soap," and "$1,000 a Week."
When the focus is on others, Danny or his stand-in often enters
as a minor character. Sometimes he is fairly prominent as in
"The Professor" or "A Lesson in History," but more often he is
the observant narrator or a soundingboard for other characters,
as in "After the Sun Has Risen" and "On a Train to Rome." In
a dozen stories Danny appears only in the conversation, thoughts,
or dreams of others—notable instances are in "Wedding Bells
Will Ring So Merrily," "Spring Evening," "When Boyhood
Dreams Come True," and "Shanley"—a device permitting us to
see Danny in different lights. As a result, our familiarity with

him and with his many relationships enriches the meaning of single episodes in which he appears. We who know Danny well, for instance, must be aware of his true but carefully hidden feelings in "Blisters."

Farrell uses similar tactics with other characters. Red Kelly and Willie Collins, for example, carry on through several tales and appear peripherally in others. As their circumstances change with the years, they establish the lines of their "destinies." Ed Lanson turns up at new times under other names: as Lewis Gordon in "The Life Adventurous," as Mark in "Yesterday's Love," and recently as George Raymond in *The Silence of History* and *Lonely for the Future*. The tales tighten and involve the personal relationships among Farrell's vast body of characters, yet they leave his "social universe" open and permit quick probings of unexplored regions. They add significantly to Farrell's picture of youth and age, boyish aspiration and adult acceptance, ardent love and tired middle-aged infidelity, the social life of the high-school set and young married couples, family life and the tension between the generations.

Similarly, Farrell's tales inspect the Catholic Church and the clergy, education up through the university, unions and laboring men (especially express-company workers and gas-station attendants), the politics of the ward heeler and the radical, Bohemian and literary circles, organized urban violence (sexual aggression, racial strife, criminal racketeering) and organized sports (boxing, baseball, basketball, football, tennis), and the everyday life and death of city people of numerous nationalities (Irish, Greek, Polish, Lithuanian) and of many sorts (the bum, the struggling immigrant, the white-collar serf, the chain-store magnate, to name some). Working outward from many Chicago neighborhoods—not confined to what is loosely called Farrell's "South Side"—the stories eventually reach to New York, Paris, and Europe at large. Increasingly in the last fifteen years Farrell has written of Americans in Europe, as in *French Girls Are Vicious and Other Stories* (1955), and, to some extent, about cultivated Europeans transplanted to America. Beginning with *$1,000 a Week and Other Stories* (1942), his tales often reflect his experience with publishers, writers, actors, Hollywood producers, intellectuals, and persons of some standing met in this country and abroad.

In Farrell's tales relentless pursuit of a fallible humanity is usually tempered by rare understanding, whether the quarry is a sheik "lookin 'em over" on a Chicago beach of the 1920's or a contemporary writer sardonically aware of his self-betrayal. Ben Ray Redman remarked that Farrell's stories show man as a self-deceiving creature, but as one whose self-deception is both suicidal and life-giving. Perhaps the greater emphasis lies upon that side of experience Studs represents: the frustration and blight. In a testimonial for *Calico Shoes and Other Stories* given to Vanguard Press, Evelyn Scott caught the spirit of many of Farrell's tales, particularly a large body of early ones: "In his stories, he takes what would seem the least promising material and, with a hardy honesty which rejects adornment, projects the lives of those whose minds are trite, those whose habits are unsavory, those who are banal and those who have been made perverse. . . ." Alfred Kazin has remarked that the "rude vigor" of Farrell's manner is appropriate to "the strident life that gave it birth"; and, if some readers object to a monotony of subject and treatment, others feel with S. L. Solon "that it is the monotone of a sea, not a dripping faucet."[5]

In the Preface to the 1937 volume bringing together his first three collections of tales, Farrell has written that an experience may call for translation into an anecdote, sketch, tale, novelette, or novel. His stories, accordingly, range from mere scraps of experience ("In City Hall Square") and simple sketches to *Tommy Gallagher's Crusade* (1939), a novelette about a Studs-like character of the 1930's who gives his floundering life direction through the native fascism advocated by Father Moylan, the radio priest.

Tommy, a bitter, frustrated product of the Depression, finds importance and excitement in breaking up "Red" meetings and in hawking *Christian Justice,* Father Moylan's anti-Semitic paper. As Thomas Mann wrote to Farrell on October 4, 1939, Tommy is an alarming social type; and his story is Farrell's concentrated effort to present in terms of a single character the meaning of American fascism in the 1930's (the original title was *Tommy Gallagher—American Storm Trooper).* But Tommy is perhaps too much of a type—too clear-cut an example of a major social problem—to be entirely convincing. In "The Short Story," the address that Farrell gave to the First American Writers Congress, he argued for the primacy in fiction of the sense of life and human character. Meanings must arise naturally from incidents, and incidents must be unfolded with no sacrifice of human character to ideology or to frozen form. Tommy is a consistent character who conveys terrifying meanings, but we feel that his realization as a complete human being is limited by Farrell's use of him as social illustration.

In attempting to achieve that sense of life that he values so highly in fiction, Farrell has most often, but not invariably, used the "plotless short story,"[6] the artifice of an intentionally primitive method. Not surprisingly, his tales have been profoundly affected by Chekhov's short fiction, which also emphasizes character over plot and portrays the ordinary experience of common people. In Chekhov's prodigal output Farrell found strong support for his view of short stories as "doors of understanding and awareness opening outward into an entire world."[7] About the time he read the Russian Realist in 1927, Farrell evinced what he had learned about writing fiction from Sherwood Anderson (in "Mary O'Reilley"), from Thedore Dreiser (in "The Open Road"), and from Ernest Hemingway (in "A Casual Incident"). The first two tales illustrate characteristics of his early style: both are overelaborated and tend toward "fine" descriptive writing. Learning to control his preference for metaphorical language, he rapidly developed his more objective manner of describing his characters' feelings and actions, as in the story "Jim O'Neill." Jim, recovering from his stroke, gets up in the morning to find that Lizz has gone out:

Jim shaved, his right hand tiring as he ran the straight razor over his face. He went to the kitchen, and fried eggs and bacon, and heated the pot of coffee. He carried his food to the dining-room, shoved the cluttered objects on the table aside, and sat down to eat. He glanced out of the window and saw Bob make a two-base hit. He hoped that Lizz would return shortly. He determined that he would tell her a hell of a lot. He ought to give her a good smack in the teeth. Hell, she was such a goddamn fool, praying all day in the church, until the janitors had to ask her to leave so that they could close up. Why wasn't she cleaning her house, taking care of her children, making things at home pretty and orderly—why wasn't all that as much of a prayer as kneeling down in St. Patrick's church and praying by the hour. That goddamn woman!

She still wasn't back when he finished his meal. He did not remove the dishes from the table, and went out to the kitchen to make some ham and cheese sandwiches for his lunch. He placed them, along with a slice of Ward's cake and an apple, in a newspaper, and wrapped a neat bundle.

He determined that he would tell that goddamn woman what was what.[8]

Farrell, like Hemingway and Ring Lardner, came to rely heavily upon his characters' dialogue as a means of narration in his tales and novels. Jim, earlier in his marriage, voices a mild complaint to Lizz:

"Jesus, we sure get paper on the floor here, don't we?" Jim said, seeing the paper stacked and piled under the dining-room table as he came into the room, wearing his work clothes.

"Well, Jim, I always think this. When the children are playing, I think to myself that if they got their health, it's good, and the paper they throw on the floor don't hurt the floor, not this floor full of slivers. You couldn't hurt a floor in this dump," Lizz said, standing in the door.

"The floor's sometimes so covered with papers that we can't even see it," Jim said.

"Our Lord was born in a stable. It isn't what the outside looks like. It's what the inside looks like. If your soul is clean, that counts more than if your house is. Many there are in the world with clean houses and dirty souls. And this morning, the souls in this house are clean. This morning, everyone who's old enough to in my house received the Body and Blood of our Blessed Lord," Lizz said, her voice rising in pride as she drew to the end of her declamation.

"Well, it isn't necessary to have a dirty house in order to have a clean soul," Jim said.[9]

This style has its limitations, as critics have freely asserted. Yet it permits effective, colorful contrasts of idiom, and it achieves dramatic immediacy; for character is directly exposed through the interplay of dialogue or, in other passages, through the free association of interior monologues. At its best, the style *is* the character-in-action.

Experimenting in his new style during the prolific years between 1928 and 1932, Farrell quickly came to his lyrical vein of boyhood loves and sorrows in early stories like "Autumn Afternoon" and "Helen, I Love You," and to his fiercely ironic manner in stories like "The Scarecrow" and "Two Sisters." In a manuscript "The Origin of 'The Scarecrow,'" Farrell explains that this story and others like it grew out of his collapsing romanticism and youthful indignation at cruelty practiced on others. At that time he was earnestly striving for objectivity ("letting life speak") as a technical device of style, and he was trying to use dialogue accurately for narration and atmosphere, as well as for characterization. "Strongly determined not to produce received sentiments" in his writing, he was struggling to avoid general words and to dramatize states of mind. In writing "The Scarecrow," he felt he had made "a leap into originality."

He progressively opened up the broader world of his Chicago youth in such tales as "A Jazz Age Clerk," "Spring Evening," and, somewhat later, in "Comedy Cop" and in "The Fastest Runner on Sixty-First Street." "Side Street," "They Ain't the Men They Used to Be," "The Girls at the Sphinx," and "An American Student in Paris" are examples of superior stories completed at later dates that take us outside Chicago. During the past two decades as Farrell has gone farther afield in his settings, he also has increasingly experimented with different styles. He has tried the monologue, the stream-of-consciousness, and other variants of the first-person point of view. In many of the late tales he has moved away from the vocally dramatic method of dialogue and from other methods that yield a direct impression of particularized experience; instead, he relies in them on a generalized narrative manner somewhat like the summary of a rather detached chronicler of human events. Although this manner has enabled him to condense a given character's "destiny" within a few pages while simultaneously permitting him greater freedom for authorial comment and analysis, it has meant a loss in the reader's sense of immediate participation in the experience recorded.

Farrell's stories can be heavy-handed and verbose ("Honey, We'll Be Brave"), tendentious ("Reverend Father Gilhooley"), synthetic ("Just Boys"), more skilled in portraying belching and banalities ("Thanksgiving Spirit") than nuances of feeling or thought ("The Philosopher"). Yet time and again they display his sure grasp of complex human relationships and his homing instinct for situations and values central—often elemental—in human experience. Perhaps they are most moving when he gives the illusion of dramatic objectivity to simple, compact action known from the inside. Then, most likely, truth to individual character becomes social revelation, and we feel the story as a self-sufficient unit. At the same time we seem to be confronted not by a discrete and packaged experience but by an ongoing actuality momentarily spotlighted in the stream of time. We might say with Danny O'Neill in *Boarding House Blues:* "It is not a story at all. It is an account of . . . that which has happened, has come to pass and has passed to become part of the welter of all that has happened" (210). Although Farrell has succeeded best in his novels, which impressively embody his concern with time and human emergence, his tales are an integral part of his work—and a surprising number of them are individually memorable.

CHAPTER 8

A Play, the Poems, and A Universe of Time

I *"The Mowbray Family"*

With few exceptions, Farrell's other imaginative writing also
has been in the form of prose fiction. Early in his career and
through the middle 1930's, he experimented with a play or two;
and in March, 1940, he and Hortense Alden completed the
three-act drama *The Mowbray Family,* that is included in *When
Boyhood Dreams Come True* (1946). The action of this play
takes place in New York City just before the Nazi-Soviet non-
aggression pact of 1939. The conflict anticipates the later Bernard Carr books, for conniving American Stalinists are opposed
by a young philosophy instructor who is a follower of John
Dewey and a genuine liberal. The authors' main intention, however, was to write a domestic comedy of "penthouse Bolshevism."[1]
Unfortunately, the rather inconsequential characters lack the
reality and individuality that might have made the play live.

II *The Poetry*

During 1929 and 1930, Farrell composed many poems but
published only one, "The Sacrament of Marriage," in *Poetry
World* (August, 1929), before he turned completely to the writing of prose. Several years later in a letter to James Henle he
stated his low opinion of his verse, but he confessed a continuing
urge to produce it. During the early 1960's, he surrendered to
the urge by writing new verses and revising old ones. He placed
approximately thirty of his poems in magazines and papers, and
in *The Collected Poems of James T. Farrell* (1965)[2] he brought
together forty-four verses written over four decades. Almost half
of these date from Farrell's sustained creative period of the late
1920's and early 1930's when he was first giving life to Studs
Lonigan, Danny O'Neill, and the interlocking galaxies of char-

acters around them. The remainder of the poems were written
after 1960 while Farrell was launching, during his "second career," as he termed it in a letter to John Edgar Webb of January
11, 1961, the multicycled series of thirty or more novels entitled
A *Universe of Time,* a reinterpretation of his origins and experience intended as a panorama of his times. Farrell's poetic activity appears likely to come at times of basic upheavals and
resettlings within his imaginative world.

In general, the earlier poems are more successful than the
later, although the later ones contain fewer echoes of Sherwood
Anderson's, Carl Sandburg's, and possibly Stephen Crane's verse.
The earlier poems tend to be personal expressions of doubt,
faith, love, and protest; and their tone ranges from sharp satire
to Romantic despair. Characteristically, these are forceful, roughly hewn statements of emotional turmoil or of temporary, pre-
carious balance in the poet's spiritual life. A number of them,
like "On A Possibly Trite Subject" (1929), reveal personal attitudes—usually shaped in the 1920's and carrying the authority
of time-tested acceptance—basic to his view of existence.

The poems of the 1960's, while still reflective, more often
look toward historical events and characters (Christ, François
Villon, Saint-Just, John Kennedy, Carmelitta Maracci) or backward on the author's personal past. The young man's lyrical
concern with his lonely status in a mysterious universe never
entirely disappears, but it is likely to be replaced by the aging
artist's stubborn effort to define and to follow a suitable way
of life in the face of broken dreams and "rampant, raging
mediocrity" (*CP,* 55). The older man more often than the younger
taps a vein of humor, as in "Willie Collins Speaking" (1962), a.
poem also sufficiently grim in implication, or as in "Sometimes"
(1962), light verse that does not live up to the opening promise of

> Sometimes
> I like to count the names
> Of all the dames
> That I have laid
> Away in my memory.
> (*CP,* 51)

The verse of each period has characteristic flaws. Some of the
earlier poems are given to trite imagery: in "Sights" (1927), love

blooms "like roses in June" (*CP*, 1). Others burst into unrelieved denunciation or into outraged protest, as in "Homecoming" (1929-30), where sensitivity of feeling is subordinated to the poet's blazing indignation at crassly patriotic attitudes. The poems of the 1960's are at times overexclamatory, or strangely fascinated with ringing the changes on a single word, as in "Is April Only Anguish" (1962): "the hopes that we merely hoped/ Into hopelessness" (*CP*, 42). Or they may rely too heavily in climactic positions on minor linking words and vast abstractions:

> I hear the wind, . . .
> Singing all of the world,
> Toward
> And to
> The Always Forever Silence of Silence.
> (*CP*, 39-40)

Perhaps the least effective poem of the collection is "Fragment on Greateness" (1963). In it, in a calculated flat manner, the poet's dislike of contemporary literary mediocrities comes through so innocuously that we yearn for the more slashing attacks of thirty-five years before.

On the other hand, Farrell can employ the same manner to gain unusual effects. For example, "In Vitam Aeternam" (1964) pictures Studs Lonigan—whom his earthly maker deliberately consigned to hell many years ago—risen to stuffy heavenly glory. The manner somehow suits the orthodox apotheosis of this most widely praised of Farrell's characters. The poem appears to be the novelist's sly strike at those who would consign him to the past as a "has-been" (but now a stuffily respectable one on this view) as "the author of *Studs Lonigan*." In strongly contrasting style, "Picture" (1929) is controlled imagistic verse. "Nostalgic Mood" (1929-30) captures the poet's helpless yet willful attachment to a past love:

> These slight spring winds
> Form a frail and trembling bridge
> To yesterday.
> Across their precarious stretch
> I move
> Delicate sentiments

> That shudder
> With the swinging bridge
> And their own shaking weakness.
> Yet they move relentlessly—
> At my command—
> Back to you.
>   (*CP,* 11-12)

Among other more successful efforts are "Love Poem" (1962), a sturdily simple declaration of faith in love; "Winter Evening" (1929), sensitive to serious undertones in a brief moment of social intimacy; "Midnight" (1929), a love poem bold in conception but flawed in its closing; and "Night Mood" (1930), which seems to contain the essence of Danny O'Neill in a melancholy moment.

To many readers, Farrell's verses may appeal most strongly for their faithfulness to the man and to the novelist. They expose the sensibility that has created important fiction in our time, and they reflect the dedication and strength of character that has kept Farrell, with a religious zeal, at his proper work. In the poetry we find the novelist's Romantic temperament and his susceptibility to beauty and love—sources of the equally evident hatred of all that is vulgar and defiling in his "ugly and hideous corner" of the world (*CP,* 3). Here too is his understanding of those "Who plod the streets of cities/ Reeking with murdered souls" (*CP,* 28). Even more evident, from first to last, is the man's enduring will and his hardy optimism in the face of his Naturalism. He knows very well that death ushers man into a "bare eternity" (*CP,* 31) and that while we live, "Change is law/ Beyond our wills"—(*CP,* 76). Even in our most strenuous efforts, as in his own running "breathless,/Every minute of my life" (CP, 79), he sees a ". . . sly escape from that whining why/That breaks our hearts on walls and laws of nerveless matter" (*CP,* 37).

But, as he learned these things, he became not only "angry with life" but also "angry for life" (*CP,* 78); and he later learned to accept reverses creatively, if not always stoically. Not surprisingly, then, the historical characters appearing in the poems are likely to be rebellious and courageous, to be suffering but life-bringing. As for the poet's own present condition, he sums it up, with understatement, in two phrases: "There is no shame/ In unhappiness" (*CP*, 62), and "Dreams die hard in me" (*CP*, 36).

III A Universe of Time

The three major series of novels and related tales that Farrell already has completed create in detail large patterns of experi- ence dramatizing the life and death of the self in modern America. *Yet Other Waters* (1952) and *The Face of Time* (1953) are the final novels Farrell wrote in the Bernard Carr and O'Neill- O'Flaherty series, respectively. During the next few years Farrell published collections of tales and essays but no more novels until 1961. Even before he had finished the Bernard Carr trilogy, however, he was planning a vast new cycle of novels, tales, and poems which he now calls *A Universe of Time*. He considers his new work to be the culmination of all his endeavors. Based on a reassessment of his experience, it aims to present "a rela- tivistic panorama of our times" (conversation with me, December 24, 1962). Recently Farrell has noted: "I saw a work to do, closing the gap of experience [from] Chicago—to date—the world" (letter to me, July 2, 1969). In 1960, he estimated that he would need at least twenty years to complete the series.

Farrell's original plan for *A Universe of Time* has evolved considerably over the years and is still changing. At present, he thinks the series should run to about thirty volumes. His gen- eral organization groups the books into four divisions:
    I. When Time Was Young (1924-31)
   II. Paris Was Another Time (1931-32)
  III. When Time Was Running Red (1932-37)
  IV. A Universe of Time (1937 to the present)
Farrell plans to have the action in the series occasionally dip backwards in time to the mid-nineteenth century, thus creating a countermovement to the over-all forward progression. He al- ready has selected titles for many of the individual volumes.

By May, 1969, Farrell had published six books in *A Universe of Time: The Silence of History* (1963), *What Time Collects* (1964), *When Time Was Born* (1966), *Lonely for the Future* (1966), *A Brand New Life* (1968), and *Judith* (1969).[3] With the exception of *Judith,* all of these works belong to the first division of the series, "When Time Was Young."

Farrell's method of composing these volumes and those he is now writing is similar to the method he used in creating the three parts of *Studs Lonigan*. However, it is more complex than the earlier procedure because the new cycle is more complicated than the trilogy. He composes a "continuous narrative" (letter to me, July 1, 1968) and not separately conceived entities that naturally take shape as novels when the last scene is on paper. But, in writing a "continuous narrative," Farrell does not write continuously on the same unbroken narrative sequence; instead, he keeps many sequences going at once. These sequences are segments of the over-all narrative often widely removed from each other in time of action, setting, and cast of characters; but all are conceived as parts of the ultimate structure. Farrell may keep a sequence by him for many years or have it ready for publication within a few months. When a sequence is completed to his satisfaction, he customarily constructs a novel from it. He may delete portions, rearrange scenes, or introduce episodes from another sequence before he reworks the whole.

Farrell started writing *A Universe of Time* in the early morning hours of October 21, 1958, with an account of the meeting between Eddie Ryan (his new name for the Danny O'Neill character) and Marion Healey (Danny's girl Anna Brown) in July, 1928. After completing about one hundred pages of manuscript, he decided to explore Eddie's background first; and he began a sequence showing Eddie in 1927 against the backdrop of Bohemia on Chicago's South Side. Eventually this sequence became the greater part of *Lonely for the Future*, and with the first draft of that novel Farrell achieved a breakthrough which led directly into the writing of other portions of his new cycle.

The six volumes now available suggest that *A Universe of Time*, like much of Farrell's earlier work, will be built around significant events from his personal past, especially when Eddie Ryan is center stage. (*What Time Collects* is a notable exception, for perhaps it is the least autobiographical and most "invented" of Farrell's novels.) For example, Eddie Ryan in *The Silence of History* undergoes a striking development at the University of Chicago as does Danny O'Neill in *My Days of Anger*. Also it is possible to equate numerous characters from *A Universe of Time* with differently named characters in the earlier fiction. But it may also be said that Farrell's vision of his past has matured and that the new cycle will focus in part on aspects of his past that were minimized or omitted from the earlier fiction. Thus, *A Universe of Time* will introduce novelty into the body of Farrell's work, but it will not be alien to the kinds of experience and social structures reflected in his series about Studs Lonigan, Danny O'Neill, and Bernard Carr. At many points Eddie Ryan's world will—and, indeed, already does—mesh with their worlds; and to date, at least, the new cycle reinforces the sense of unity that arises from Farrell's work as a whole.

Eddie Ryan is, of course, the key character of *A Universe of Time*. Farrell thinks of him as the integrating image of the total work, as the character to whom all other characters eventually will be directly or indirectly linked. And, Farrell explained in his letter to Sheldon Binn of March 5, 1963, "what went on before Eddie, and/or in his absence [will be] linked up with Eddie's life in some way, important or not—important—to Eddie." But Farrell was quick to add that the world of his new cycle, although relating to Eddie, will not be constrictive but rather panoramic, centrifugal, and open: "The world is bigger than Eddie. Through a pattern of associations, many characters are introduced, and many paths are traced. From book to book, the past shall grow, and change, and grow and swell." The initial volumes of the series, he believes, have created "a concrete past" out of which "succeeding events of the books will emerge." The past becomes a living factor in the changing present; and "From book to book, all of this will grow, and as it grows, the panoramic picture I am creating will be enlarged."[4]

Thus, although *A Universe of Time* will interlock with his earlier work, Farrell intends for it to yield a more comprehensive view of experience than any of his other series. He likes to speak of the new cycle as his *"Comédie humaine."* Presumably, its interpretation of modern life will explicitly reinforce the large patterns of meaning that emerge from the interrelated series on Studs Lonigan, Danny O'Neill, and Bernard Carr if Farrell realizes his purpose. For he maintained, in a conversation of December 24, 1962, with me, that the basic themes of *A Universe of Time* will be "man's creativity and his courageous acceptance of impermanence." He also wrote to the editor of the Pioneer Press on September 7, 1960: "I shall not [see], and have not so far seen my characters in terms of heroes and villains, but as human beings, [who] carry their humanity through the disappearing minutes. It is my hope, and in a non-chauvinist sense, to assert to the world, that we in America can conceive great creative projects, and possess the discipline and the will to carry these through to the end, working many hours through the solitude of many nights. . . . I hope to . . . touch what I regard as the untapped creativity that sleeps in many, if it be not awakened. In giving, I seek to give us, ourselves and our years to the memory of men." Farrell's point about creativity brings us back to the importance of Eddie Ryan; for "the central theme" of creativity in the series "is not only affirmed. It is and will be lavishly exhibited by the narrator all through. . . ."[5] If Farrell's explanation of his intentions sometimes borders on the melodramatically grandiose—an impression not contradicted by the imposing titles of some of the series volumes—his conception is nevertheless vast and his plan of execution impressive.

A. *The Silence of History.* Farrell has stated in a letter to me of July 2, 1969, that he wrote *The Silence of History* (1963) because "I needed a work that would carry and predicate a vast series." The concentration of this novel on Eddie's growth at a time crucial to his later development tends to substantiate Farrell's claim.

In this work, which explores the period from June, 1925, to July, 1926, in Eddie Ryan's life, Eddie is a student at the University of Chicago; and his experience there resembles Danny O'Neill's in *My Days of Anger.* Yet *The Silence of History,* initiating a new series, differs significantly from the O'Neill-O'Flaherty novels. In those books Danny gradually emerges from his family and neighborhood, the dense social setting that Farrell gives a life of its own. Members of Danny's family especially are well-developed characters whose personal histories are knit into the general action, which moves outward from Danny into the life of the city.

In contrast, *The Silence of History* has a centripetal movement. It centers on an inner action, the "undramatic drama"[6] of mind and spirit extending over one year and leading Eddie to a decision that he knows will demand personal sacrifice and risk. To be sure, other characters important in his life appear in concentrated counterpoint to him; Farrell spaces their capsule histories throughout the book. But their stories primarily serve to sharpen the focus on Eddie's individuality—he asserts that he is "no one's type, no one's allegory, no one's illustration of any kind of preconception" (367). They point up his existential affirmation of uniqueness that is also implicit in the critical decision he must make. In a sense, *The Silence of History* is an answer to those critics who have questioned Farrell's ability to make man's spirit as powerful a determining force as he has made the shaping "conditions" of life.

Eddie is aware that knowledge is his key to future success, that it alone will enable him to erase "the stamp of inferiority" he bears from the dispirited social world of his origins (91). Thus his well-paying job in a service station is indispensable, for it offers favorable study conditions and money for tuition. Yet, acting from compelling impulse, he gives up his job, and the action assumes symbolic importance to him. He sees it as "an assertion, an irrevocable step toward freedom"—his way of saying "No" to the sacred values of the acquisitive society that he reads about in R. H. Tawney's writing (366). His decision, we learn, is made in the interest of his growing "sense of Destiny," and, to Eddie, destiny comes to mean "a fate, to be lived with and to be fought," that has "a time schedule of eternity" (49).

The essential action is, therefore, Eddie's spiritual growth during the year before his decision. He progresses from the ideal of business success, which had saturated his boyhood home, to the idea of self-realization that will lead him "deeply into life" down "a long road . . . far beyond the range of his vision" (117, 167). Offended by his personal past, Eddie establishes through education a relationship to a wider and nobler reality than any he had known before. For Eddie, that reality comes to include mankind's public, meaningful past (he reads history avidly) and its brighter future, in which he wants to truly count. At this time, his imagined personal future is vague and grandiose. He is still trying to find himself, so that he may, perhaps, break the silence of history. He fears the anonymity that befalls most men, including especially, it seems to him, the Irish as a nation.

Eddie's new awareness makes him treasure time; boredom becomes impossible. Walter Pater's "Conclusion" to *Studies in the History of the Renaissance* speaks to him powerfully, saying that "each moment should have value and quality" (175). "And

he wouldn't live the pitiful sacrifice to the gods that be. . . .
Before they died, men should live and feel the world as a
quickened pulse of love and joy and whatever was beautiful
in life" (273). But men, Eddie learns, nourish "a great wrong-
ness" inside, "like a fever that burned them when they thought
they were cool. They were hurting themselves, and leading
themselves into a swamp where the germs of their own illness
proliferated" (269). Eddie begins to feel a "slow-growing anger"
(269). His intensity is well reflected in two first-person chapters
in which he and the omniscient author merge. It is as though
the developing self bursts through the anonymous third-person
form to express the personal inner pressures in their original
urgency.

Likewise, the theme of individual growth explains Farrell's
excursions into the past history and the psychology of other
characters, whose directions in life become variations on the
idea of Destiny versus Success. Mr. Wood, Eddie's boss, lives
for advancement in business; and Joe Deacon, Eddie's supervisor, is the commercial flunkey, frustrated, envious, aggressive.
Peter Moore, Eddie's good friend, is sensitive but without the
personal strength to avoid compromise. Eddie's grandmother,
Grace Hogan Dunne, is driven by poverty from Ireland to seek
a new life in a new world—a search Eddie repeats on the level
of intellect. Like Eddie, Professors Carleton and Carson are
committed to the world of mind—but under the shelter of a university. Eddie's uniqueness among these characters is that he
alone will follow the artist's road, although he does not yet
fully know this. But he does learn that to win out he must cultivate "not only knowledge, but courage, will, determination,
and defiance—without these he was lost" (351).

B. *Lonely for the Future.* Eddie Ryan's past is also explored
in *Lonely For the Future* (1966). The action opens in Chicago
on March 27, 1927, some eight months after Eddie's decision in
The Silence of History to give up his job, and it closes in mid-
July as Eddie and his friend George Raymond begin hitchhiking
to New York City. In the earlier novel Eddie's role was central,
but in this book he shares the stage with George and Alec Mc-
Gonigle, another friend, each of whom Farrell will feature in
later novels. All three young men are in their early twenties.
They become implicated in the affairs of the Bohemian Forum,

a night spot located just across Washington Park from Eddie's home. This discotheque of the prohibition 1920's attracts students, clerks, stenographers, homosexuals, and, in general, young people "on the make." It is a pale copy of the flourishing Bohemian hangout on Chicago's Near North Side called the "Sour Apple" or the "Wild Onion" in Farrell's fiction. With the help of Alec McGonigle, the club is run by two visionaries: Wilbert Wilmer (who dreams of founding a colony in the Ozark Mountains to be governed according to the principles of Herbert Spencer's philosophy) and old John Mason (Bill Bailey of *Boarding House Blues*), a kindly, brokendown Socialist who once ran for mayor of Cleveland. Farrell primarily presents the loves, intrigues, and power struggles within the Bohemian Forum and its offspring, the Slow-Down Club, in order to contrast the values of Alec, George, and Eddie.

Alec, the bright son of a broken home, still carries heavy psychological burdens of guilt and social inferiority from his boyhood. An intellectual rebel like Eddie and George, he cannot, however, accept the risk of burning his bridges to the past; he wants the status and the power of the world that has rejected him. Presumably Alec will return to law school after Eddie and George leave for New York. George, on the other hand, is a reembodiment of Ed Lanson from *Ellen Rogers* and *Boarding House Blues*. Just as charming and aggressively wicked as Ed Lanson, George "muscles in" on the Forum proprietors for the money and the excitement. He has, however, no permanent ties to anything or anyone; for he considers himself a superman who is not only beyond good and evil but also beyond a steady occupation. He is a great reader of Nietzsche and cultivates other persons to "use" them any way he can. George flourishes on disruption and ruin: he supplies the Forum with blinding washtub gin, encourages the advances of the homosexual Riggs in order to humiliate him, and mercilessly beats a club member after seducing his girl. Eddie, who wants to be courageous, is attracted by George's undoubted daring, but he begins to see that George takes risks only for the joy of destruction, that he cares for nothing else.

"But Eddie Ryan did care, and he was determined to make others care."[7] Like Alec, he saw his life as a struggle to overcome an inferiority complex, and "the bridges Eddie felt he must burn

led not only to all that he had rejected, but also to a past in
which he believed he had been a failure" (204). It is important
to realize that, less than two weeks before the opening action of
the novel, Eddie had dropped out of the University of Chicago
with the intention of making his way as a writer or going under
in the attempt. This second crucial decision within a year is an
important step in Eddie's effort to throw away crutches and to
walk alone. With the recklessness born of his new-found intellectualism and his deep-seated sense of not being loved, he
thinks, like George, that he wants to cast off all authority and
live beyond good and evil. His motto is "All Things Are Nothing
to Me" (106); and, like Max Stirner's egoist, he would like to
say: "I, this nothing, shall put forth my creations from myself"
alone.[8]

But, in truth, Eddie cannot dissolve the world—either its reality
or its values—in his ego. George believes "the world is really as
if it were the world we think it is—it's inside our heads." But
Eddie answers: "Rocks aren't as if they were rocks. They are
rocks . . . they'll go through a window if we throw them. . . . We
can have illusions or false notions about it, but we still are in a
world which is what it is" (147). Whereas George is contemptuous of others and exploits them, Eddie is unable not to pity such
persons as Riggs the homosexual and old John Mason. And, although Eddie could not remain consistent with his stated views
and still morally disapprove of George's selfish use of people, "he
found that he didn't like to see it done" (114).

Eddie, in short, is already very much the Humanist and the
Naturalist. He acutely feels "the oppression of time" (127) in
two ways: as a would-be writer who fears he may die without
having written anything valuable, and as a thinker who sees
that "all men are caught in a trap of time" and nothingness (148).
But for Eddie the ultimate purposelessness of all human life intensifies the need to find order and meaning through art while
life may last. He berates himself for wasting time at the Forum
when he should be writing. Eddie also is still romantic, immature, naïve—for example, he had expected to meet people at the
Forum genuinely interested in books and ideas—but we see him
learning, losing some illusions about Bohemia, and judging others
with growing maturity. Compared to the manipulating George
and to the scheming Alec, he is the spectator. His relatively

passive role in the novel is appropriate to one who is unsure of his acceptance by others and who wants to write.

In *Lonely for the Future* Farrell came back to a central nerve of autobiography in his fiction. As the novel closes, Eddie leaves for New York because he felt he had to, just as Danny O'Neill felt in *My Days of Anger.* Their psychology is much the same. Likewise, *Lonely for the Future* is closely connected with *Boarding House Blues* and with *New Year's Eve/1929.* In those novels, Danny O'Neill is a little older and more mature than Eddie Ryan is in 1927; but, like Eddie, he is still intent on winning success as a writer. *Lonely for the Future,* however, reveals a new segment of the autobiographical hero's life as it also stresses the background and experience of two of his closest friends, Alec and George.

C. *When Time Was Born.* Major themes of *The Silence of History* and *Lonely for the Future* permeate *When Time Was Born* (1966). Originally this prose poem of several thousand words was an integral part of the sequence that became *What Time Collects* (1964), but Farrell removed it and later published it separately. *When Time Was Born* has been called Farrell's rewriting of Chapter 1 of Genesis and the Garden of Eden story. Poles apart in manner from Whitman's "Song of Myself," it nevertheless is Farrell's Whitmanesque celebration of the creation and creativity, of "the undying wonder of the world,"[9] the incessant surge of existence toward more complex states of awareness and being as the self interacts with others and with the world as experienced. Death, the vestibule to new life, is put in counterpoint to man's capacity for idealism and dream; and Paradise, the state of sensuous, nonconceptualized happiness in which Adam had no need even to "know what to say" to Eve (63), is soon replaced by the world of ideation, labor, suffering, desire, and universal procreation. Man's creativity is seen as springing from his weaknesses and his need for another person, and love in all its forms is linked to the growth of personal awareness—the strengthening of "the inner wind of consciousness" (30) —and to the beat and pace of time itself. *When Time Was Born* is a lyrical and whimsical statement of underlying themes in Farrell's *A Universe of Time.*

D. *What Time Collects.* In 1964 Farrell brought out *What Time Collects,·* the second novel of his series to appear. The present time in this work is approximately 1924 to 1925; but, through long stretches of the action, Farrell takes us back as far as the 1870's to explore the antecedents of his chief characters. The setting is not Chicago but Valley City, a fictional Midwestern town patterned on Indianapolis; and no characters appearing in *The Silence of History* or in *Lonely for the Future* are so much as mentioned. Nevertheless, *What Time Collects* parallels Eddie Ryan's story in its concern with the formation of a "decision to make some kind of leap into life"[10] in pursuit of self-liberation. This theme comes into focus through the character of Anne Duncan Daniels, a girl in her early twenties. What time slowly "collects" in Anne is precisely the strength of will to emerge from the "scummy pool" (399) of her marriage to Zeke Daniels and eventually to break radically with her past. Divorced and defiant at the conclusion of the novel, Anne will presumably leave Valley City for Chicago where, perhaps, "her feelings would be new, she would be new, all brand-new" (130). Neither Anne nor the reader can predict the outcome of her future struggle for fulfillment; but in this novel she clearly belongs with other seekers like Danny O'Neill and Eddie Ryan: all three develop the self-knowledge and the courage that permit them to act decisively in response to deep individual needs.

Before her marriage to Zeke Daniels, Anne lived with her puritanical, widowed mother and worked as a waitress, having dropped out of high school after little more than two years. When she was thirteen, Anne rejected her mother's fear of love: Mrs. Duncan preaches that men are no better than animals because "the Devil was in man's britches; and he gave a woman only pain and tribulation" (12). Although Anne is an attractive, reasonably popular girl, she constantly senses the aimless drift of her life, a feeling partly rooted in her growing "sexual desperation" (67). Zeke initially appeals to Anne because of his apparent strength; but, having successfully foiled his sexual aggression on their first date, she knows she is the stronger. Leaving Zeke that night, Anne stumbles on the porch steps and sprains her ankle. The accident signalizes "a sense of new importance, and an intuition that she had won some kind of victory over Zeke Daniels" (46). She uses her sprained ankle, in fact, to win Zeke as a husband. Submitted to constant indignity in her marriage, Anne eventually gains the upper hand, and again a disabling accident, this time Zeke's stumble on a staircase, signalizes her triumph. She breaks out of a sexual and psychological slavery that had imprisoned her in an ugly union: the mysterious "something accumulating in her" (117) that originally impelled her to marry Zeke continues to nourish her determination to make still another "leap into life" (118).

Anne's husband Zeke is an insurance salesman in his father's prosperous agency. During Sunday church services he likes to please the "hens" by powerfully booming out the hymns, but mostly he aims to please the "chicks," who need "something besides the Lord" (39). A lover of "nooky-wooky" (143), Zeke is the self-proclaimed champion "collector of coose" (144) in Valley City, a hobby he continues to indulge after his marriage. One of the crudest personalities among Farrell's males, he caricatures the worst features of Studs. He is spoiled and egocentric. He is an expert in applying the double standard, and beyond his prejudices he is mindless. He values women only for their sexual use and men as an admiring audience for his sexual boasting.

But Zeke is a monster partly because he is a wretched victim. His crippled self is the end result of "the whole loveless heritage of the Daniels family" (400)—what time collected for him. Praised but unloved by his parents, he parodies their "selfishness and frustrated sensuality" (400) in his preoccupation with sex. His life outwardly distorts what was "hidden and denied" (400) in them. The rage he turns against Anne represents a lifelong accumulation of a "concentrated fury against himself, against his mother, his father, his family . . . as much as against Anne" (409), who crumbles his last defenses against the truth about himself. Thus what Anne escapes in leaving Zeke is the "pitiless banality, pitiless emptiness, pitiless hate and pitiless loneliness" (399) that unknowingly she had assumed when she took his name.

Zeke, like Studs, symbolizes a spiritual malady in his society; and the ills of the solid, middle-class Protestants of Valley City are surprisingly similar to those of the Lonigans in Chicago. Zeke's father Tom and his friends are successful business men who "have attained their peak at the dead center of mediocrity" (187). Smug and sentimental, they think "their kind formed the solid human foundations which make the edifice of the United States of America the very greatest in the world" (190). So long

as they can dominate, they are friendly and neighborly; and they
want to be liked. But they express their insecurities by joining
the Ku Klux Klan, as does Zeke. Living "in the historic shadow
of the pioneers" (185) and inheriting a religion "which drilled
fear of their instincts into the basis and bottom of their beings"
(190), they endure their stale existence by indulging in dreams
of courageous adventure and lustful sexual fantasies. Like Sinclair Lewis' George F. Babbitt and his friends in Zenith, they
have "a conceited assurance of moral superiority, and a hardened
pride that the Word, final and unchangeable, had been given
unto their kind" (190). In this society the women tend to take
on the spiritual coloration of their husbands. Zeke's mother
Frances, whose mind Farrell explores at great length, is much
stronger than her son and her husband; and she understands far
more than they do. But she too is the deformed product of a loveless marriage between her puritanical mother and her pitilessly
cold, commercial father.

What Time Collects is an ambitious work. It effectively adds
new "panels" to Farrell's picture of America. Most of the book
is an intricately contrived flashback of 365 pages that probes the
family histories of the Duncans and the Daniels. As Farrell proceeds, he displays an exceptional understanding of his characters'
values and their sexual fantasies. Consequently, the long perspective he takes on the heritage of Anne and Zeke lends social
depth and psychological credibility to his picture of their relationship. His flashback supplies a marked propulsive power to
the action that makes up the thin line of the advancing present
in this tale.

Yet the novel disappoints in two respects. First, Farrell's portrayal of his characters depends too heavily upon his running
narrative commentary; and analysis largely replaces dramatic
action. Second, both the logic and the tendency of the story re-
quire that Anne and Zeke be the climactic characters who carry
Farrell's meaning; but neither engages our full interest because
of his or her relative thinness. Their origins are fully explained,
yet in themselves Zeke and Anne lack the complex density of
Frances Daniels' character. Thus the novel not only conveys a
disproportion but also arouses expectations that are not met in
terms of adequate characterization.

E.   *A Brand New Life.* We learn considerably more about Anne Duncan Daniels in *A Brand New Life* (1968), the fourth novel in Farrell's current series and the one that brings Anne to the periphery of Eddie Ryan's world. Following her divorce from Zeke, Anne goes to Chicago in February, 1928; and we see her during a four-month period winning her brand new life and new loves—and, for Anne, these are nearly identical pursuits. We see relatively little of Chicago through Anne's eyes, but two old residents, Anne's successive lovers the brothers Roger and George Raymond, bring the action from the bedroom to the city streets. Thus we are in familiar territory, ranging from the North Side (Lincoln Park, the Edgewater Beach Hotel, the Lake Michigan shore, and the Paragon dance hall) to the South Side (Jackson Park, Sixty-third Street, and the University of Chicago neighborhood). The brothers also roam the downtown area, patronizing such places as the central library, the Art Institute, Henrici's, and Harding's restaurant on Wabash Avenue. From the open air of double-decker busses on Michigan Avenue to the secrecy of Prohibition speakeasies, Farrell unobtrusively introduced Chicago of the late 1920's as he moved his characters about.

To Anne, the new life Chicago offers is the opportunity to find "the real Anne"[11] through love. Long deprived of sex in Valley City after her break with Zeke, she is ready for romantic adventure; and, in fact, she is more than a sexual match for Roger and George combined. Anne is formidable. Lacking a strong imagination, she nevertheless is natural, honest, down-to-earth, a "dangerous female" (169), as Roger only partially realizes. When her friend Fay romanticizes an affair by locating it in a "house of assignation," Anne wonders: "What does it matter where you do it?" (153). As Farrell commented in a letter to Mrs. Jane P. Loving of September 14, 1968, "Anne is trapped in her own commonness"—a commonness of mind and conduct. But her sexual insatiability expresses her strong and understandable need for love; beyond that, she is independent and knowledgeable in very female ways. Despite her lowly origins, she feels she is as good as anyone.

After several weeks of frantic sexual indulgence with Roger, Anne realizes that her deeper need is an articulate communication that will bring out "the real herself, the person she had to have Roger know" (181). Anne, who also needs spiritual in-

timacy, resents Roger's remoteness; she sees "how much went on
separately in their lives and minds. . . . They were waiting, waiting for life" (189). Ironically, the literal-minded Anne scarcely
recognizes the same trap of spiritual isolation plastically expressed in Lorado Taft's *Solitude of the Soul,* Roger's favorite
sculpture in the Art Institute. This work depicts four naked
figures, "sad-looking and linked by their hands," but each one is
"alone and separated from the others" (54), much the way
Roger, Anne, and their friends feel at the climax of a strip-poker
party. The sense of loneliness felt by Studs Lonigan and Danny
O'Neill, as well as by Roger and George Raymond, is nevertheless alive in Anne. Her tragedy in *A Brand New Life* is that
neither of her lovers really wants her or anyone else to breach
the spiritual walls behind which he feels secure; and, by herself,
Anne is inadequate to the task. Presumably, her search for a satisfying, truly mutual love will continue, for Farrell plans to bring
her and Alec McGonigle (from *Lonely for the Future)* together
in a later novel.

Roger Raymond is a successful salesman who has made his
peace with business demands—or with Babbitry, as his younger
brother George likes to think. Yet by nature Roger is introspective and secretive, a dilettante in the arts who is incurably
literary and Romantic in his reactions. He lacks the sadistic
pleasure George takes in destruction, but he shares with George
a sense of superiority over others. George, who is about a year
older than he is in *Lonely for the Future,* is more adept than
ever at living off others; and he has also refined his techniques
of seduction. He knows unerringly whom to choose and exactly
when in order to squeeze out the last drop of wicked pleasure:
he steals Anne from Roger, who was supporting him at the time.
Thus Anne's misfortune is to be vulnerable twice over to the
Raymond charm and mentality. As the novel ends, she believes
she has found happiness with George in her second new Chicago
life, and she willingly pays the rent for their apartment. She is
unaware that George already has discarded her in his thoughts.[12]
Anne is George's victim no less than Ellen Rogers is the victim
of Ed Lanson, but Anne has a resilience that Ellen lacked.

Eddie Ryan does not appear in *A Brand New Life,* although
we learn that he has returned from New York to Chicago. Yet he
plays a part in the novel, because from time to time, he enters

the thoughts of Roger and George; and, through their conversation, even Anne becomes aware of him. This indirect presentation of Eddie follows the technique Farrell used with Danny
O'Neill and other characters in earlier novels and tales. It reminds us again of Farrell's intention to have Eddie provide the
autobiographical image central to *A Universe of Time,* and it
adds to our view of Eddie's life in the 1920's. It is evident that
Eddie and George have grown apart following a period when
they worked together for a Chicago undertaker earlier in the
year. George and Roger recognize Eddie's strength of purpose
and his compassion for people "trapped in their own . . . wordless
pathos become poetry" (79), his obsession with time and impermanence—all qualities that comment on the more frantic and
passion-bound interests of Anne and her two lovers. Eddie's
presence, in short, adds a helpful perspective in a novel that
convincingly portrays its subject but that is narrower in its range
of dramatic interest and variety than are most of Farrell's books.

   F. *Judith.* Although Eddie Ryan is on the fringes of the action
in *A Brand New Life,* he is at the heart of the short novel *Judith*
(1969), Eddie's account of his affair with a concert pianist in
the 1950's. Farrell wrote *Judith* not long before he conceived *A
Universe of Time,* and he annexed it to the series a decade later
(in the first version of *Judith,* Eddie was called Danny O'Neill).
Inevitably, the annexation seems arbitrary because of the thirty-
year gap in Eddie's experience between *Lonely for the Future*
and *Judith.* In the latter work Eddie is not a struggling youth
but an established middle-aged writer. Moreover, the style and
form of *Judith* do not call to mind the earlier books of the series.
Eddie's controlled first-person narrative, terse and direct, moves
swiftly and logically from beginning to end. Essentially, it is
Eddie's recall of what happened and his inferences therefrom, a
chronicle liberally intermixed with generous passages of dialogue
that provide still another level of dramatic immediacy. Even
though the first-person narrative of remembered experience is
not commonly found in Farrell's work at any time, in its direct
impact and in its lively pace *Judith* recalls much of Farrell's
fiction in the 1930's. Farrell perhaps intended *Judith* to demonstrate that his character Eddie Ryan, the professional author,
knows how to write.

In *Judith*, Eddie tells his story in mid-1958 when he is fifty-four years old. He had known Judith since 1947, but his memories naturally converge on the years 1951-54 during which he and Judith had three affairs, each lasting about two months more or less. Judith is an internationally recognized pianist and is especially famous for her Bach interpretations. She grew up on Chicago's West Madison Street, a child prodigy in an impoverished family. Like Eddie, she was attracted to New York. Aided by scholarships and a rigidly imposed self-discipline, she achieved the excellence and fame she hungered for, but only at the cost of "love, warmth, closeness" (20).[13] "The Piano had grown into her life," and finally it had claimed her "most intimate feelings, her dreams, her capacity for love, for giving, the justification of her life . . ." (17). Thus psychologically Judith could not "give herself fully" to a man (28). Although she is a vital artist, Eddie senses "a vacancy, a center of emptiness" at the core of her being (17); and he ultimately sees her as "a wistful creature" who "wanted to be in love and to be loved" (59)—but who wanted a career more.

As Eddie recognizes, he and Judith are alike in many ways; but his remarks about her may apply to himself more often than he realizes. From similar backgrounds, both are hard-driving, successful artists in mid-career who, as Eddie says, "had not won in our careers because of the inspiration of love" (61) but who, nevertheless, crave love (Eddie's affairs with Judith are sandwiched in between his two marriages and are spiced with contemporary affairs involving Moira in America and Jeanette in France). Eddie comments that "we had both hemmed ourselves within our separate loneliness," inevitable for the artist; and he wonders why "neither of us had trusted our love, our feeling for one another" (57).

The answer is clear: the obstacle to a more permanent relationship is the inescapable contradiction each feels between the demands of his art and the demands of love. As Eddie says, "I did not want to become dependent on her. She seemed to feel the same way. We had often spoken of permanence; we both placed our work above all else. . . . We could not help but think in terms of what would be good for our careers . . ." (28). In some respects the affair, regarded simply as an affair, is ideal: manageably passionate, not too demanding, it is a release that enables them to "retain the clarity and discipline" (18) essential to their arts, and a diversion from labor that fits tidily into their schedules. Eddie senses the comic aspect of such an arrangement, and as he proceeds with his narrative larger comic patterns appear.

For example, these lovers who are so well matched physically and temperamentally are at variance in the ebb and flow of their feelings for each other. They are inadvertently on an emotional seesaw. When one is capable of declaring for love, the other is not. But the reader soon realizes that thoughts of "permanency" (29) which recurrently beguile Eddie—and, he thinks, Judith—are delusory. Farrell has written in a letter to me of March 14, 1969, that the theme of *Judith* appears to be "Artists and Egos go on"; and he might have added: "Let the chips of love fall where they may."

Much of the effectiveness of *Judith* lies in Eddie's excellence as narrator. By and large, he leaves the impression of being factual, accurate, honest, sensitive. After leaving Judith one evening, he muses:

In a sense, a dream of my youth was being fulfilled. Two artists, falling in love. But the reality was different from my dream. It was not disillusioning but it was different. Judith and I were not depending on each other, growing together, with our work intertwined, living almost every minute in unison. We were quite independent of each other and did not feed on each other's nature for our work. . . . I thought idly. A writer and a concert pianist. This love affair was so different from how such an affair might be imagined by others. But I was thinking of the cliches and banalities of love, which were silly. Things were very simple with Judith. (*Judith*, 23-24)

Eddie sees the affair for what it is and also in the context of his youthful romanticism.

Farrell carefully constructs the impression of his narrator's reliability. For example, Eddie corrects his sloppy, initial statement about his feeling for some lines from Francis Thompson's "The Hound of Heaven"; he recognizes his lack of warmth and closeness, as well as Judith's, and he admits to a mixture of relief and regret when Judith is not free to see him one evening. We feel that in telling of the affair Eddie really wants to be true to his feelings and to the quality of the relationship as he knows it (we never get inside Judith's mind). To be sure, he may be deluding himself when he thinks that Judith is genuinely in love with him and is ready to declare that love. Even so, Eddie is quick to admit his delusions when he recognizes them as such. And, if his judgment about Judith's love is a delusion, as seems likely from all that we know of her character, it nevertheless truly expresses with an additional comic touch the male vanity of Eddie, who must "go on" as artist and ego, no matter how women and affairs may come and go.

G. *Invisible Swords. Invisible Swords,* Farrell's twenty-third novel,[14] is a story of congenital retardation in a child and its effects upon the parents. Although the story has no direct link with either the characters or the actions of previously published volumes in *A Universe of Time* series, it is apparent that the writer Tod Johnson of *Invisible Swords* and Eddie Ryan of *Judith* both reflect aspects of Farrell the mature novelist. In its concern with a harsh type of biological tragedy, *Invisible Swords* does relate to Farrell's *Father and Son, The Face of Time,* and *This Man and This Woman*—three novels which carefully record steps in an organic deterioration that ends either in death (Jim O'Neill; Tom O'Flaherty) or in madness (Peg Callahan).

The action of the novel covers three years, from mid-1946 to June, 1949. Bill and Ethel Martin, aged forty-two and thirty-nine, respectively, in 1946, are upper-middle-class New Yorkers and the parents of five-year-old Jackie. Bill, the capable but passive senior editor of the publishing firm of Lionel and Wardman, is dominated by Ethel, whose sensitivity and strength of mind, together with her capacity for determined action, suggest that her role as housewife and mother must inevitably fail to satisfy her. As they sit together on the porch of their rented summer home late on a warm, moonlit night in 1946, Ethel is keenly aware of the slow erosion of their marriage, its humdrum quality spiced only by her frequent emotional outbursts. The soft moonlight on nearby low mountains speaks to them of "some universal serenity" (31), a depth of "happiness . . . and harmony" (34) they both seek. To Bill's shocked surprise, Ethel bluntly asserts: "We can save our family and be happier, if we have another child" (39). *Invisible Swords* is the deeply ironic sequel to that assertion.

Billy is born in September, 1947. Except for a correctable
deformity of the feet he is a beautiful child who seems to be
normal. His angelic appearance when he sleeps, indeed, suggests
a spiritual perfection, and not until the following spring do
Ethel's repressed fears turn to sudden terror with her first glimpse
of Billy's "idiot grin" (521). At twenty-one months, Billy is turned
over to a kind Brooklyn couple for custodial care while he awaits
admission to an institution for the hopelessly retarded. The novel
spins out those twenty-one months of Billy's undeveloped life
through a long series of short scenes in which the omniscient
author explores the daily experience of Bill and Ethel. We observe their resurgent love at Billy's birth, the mounting exaspera-
tion at continuing daily trials (Billy's slow eating habits), the
growing anxiety (Billy's rolling head, his vacant expression),
the accelerating search for medical reassurance and aid, the
eventual anguished realization and questioning—"Why? Why
us?" (709)—the rage and guilt, the final despair, and the deadness of a marriage that mechanically continues, at least temporarily, as may be seen in the novel's effective ending.

Farrell's picture of Ethel under stress is particularly memorable. Proud and quite feminine in her intuitive perceptions and
in her fierce and tender love, she forcefully expresses her growing sense of loss and the mounting horror in her life. Suspicious,
impatient, sarcastic, accusatory, irrational, she strikes out repeatedly at her bewildered husband, who cannot fully compre-
hend her depth of feeling and the source, in her love, of her
fear and rage. Ethel's loneliness, her immersion in self, her growing contempt for men and their world, and an increasing strain
of paranoia link her with Peg Callahan of *This Man and This
Woman*.

On the other hand, Bill, who is less perceptive than Ethel, has
a limited capacity to feel and experience. A frustrated novelist, he
retains his somewhat naive college faith in "an undercurrent in
life, moving forwards to create a world of truth" (110) which he,
as a hardworking editor—"an intelligent drudge" (76), he once
muses—likes to think he helps along. Bill is rational, fair-minded,
decent, and self-controlled, but he is unaware of the vanity and
smug self-esteem at the core of his character. Although his suffering over Billy is real, he uses the salve compounded of self-pity

and self-justification. He tends to evade the reality of his life
through sentimental regrets of what-might-have-been.

The portrait of Bill opens up a new area of experience in Farrell's fiction: the world of New York publishing. We participate
in Bill's labors over manuscripts; his conferences with authors
and with Joe Lionel, his boss; the business lunches and cocktail
parties; meetings of the firm's editorial board; the consternation
among old-line houses occasioned by the paperback explosion;
and the publishers' dominating concern with sales and profits.
One of Bill's friends is Tod Johnson, a talented and established
author on Lionel and Wardman's list since the 1930's. Then Tod
had been "a real white hope" (288) of American letters, but his
more recent novels have proved disappointing. Sales of his books
have steadily declined, and he is in debt to his publisher. His
work, in fact, is widely criticized as pessimistic and out of date.
Yet he refuses to modify his "ideal . . . to let life speak—to catch
those scenes where you know that life is speaking through you"
(289). Bill maintains that Tod has elements of greatness, but a
junior editor remarks of Tod's writing: "Younger people feel that
realism, naturalism is shallow—it isn't for them. They've gone
beyond it" (486).

Farrell cleverly employs a crisis in Tod Johnson's life to simultaneously satirize the commercial bias of American publishing
and to drive home the overpowering despair brought on by the
severe retardation of one's child. Tod's new manuscript, *Caro-
line's Destiny,* is a searing story of his young wife's slow death
from cancer—a blow from fate comparable in its unrelieved hopelessness to the blow that struck Bill and Ethel. In his novel, Tod
dared to grapple honestly with the meaning of the experience—
the "naked tragedy" (292)—even though the effort tore him apart
as he wrote. This very honesty of vision is almost too much for
Bill, who barely can struggle through the manuscript. "He did
not want to face his life and Tod's novel would force him to do
so" (811). Thus Farrell joins two plot lines at a moment of crisis
for both Bill and Tod, as Bill, in despair over Billy, tries to read
and judge the novel in which Tod has invested so much of his
emotional being.

Eventually Bill recommends against the publication of *Caro-
line's Destiny:* although the novel is powerful, it is too depressing—in effect, too honest—and so will not sell. For this "honest"

opinion, Bill is rewarded by Joe Lionel. Just as Bill evades direct self-examination, and just as Joe Lionel evades articulating the dread meanings of existence, so they both find "good" critical reasons to justify their rejection of Tod's novel. Bill is not strong enough to honestly engage the starkest human realities, either in life or in literature. His evasion and Tod Johnson's tormented grappling with his experience effectively suggest two ways of meeting the horror that lurks behind the beauty of little Billy.

CHAPTER 9

Conclusion

I *Influences*

The creative potential inherent in Farrell's "plebeian" origin was basic to his career. An exceptional and sensitive person, Farrell was born into a situation that generated deeply felt responses eventually expressed through his writing. His native environment profoundly affected the character of his insight, what he wrote, and the way he wrote it. In his writing, he has said, the cheese is more important than the knife that slices it—his early education in human nature more important than intellectual and literary influences. At twenty, he was still intellectually naïve and comparatively unread; but his knowledge of human beings and his experience of frustration and tragedy had been extraordinarily rich. At twenty-five, as a university student who had rejected much of his past, he was beginning to "slice the cheese"— in his first stories. Since then, what Farrell's writing has said about spiritual poverty and self-fulfillment, acquiescence and angry revolt, hopeless traps and escapes to freedom, has been conditioned by his changing insights into his origins, even though his subjects often take him far from Chicago's South Side. So keenly did Farrell feel the city's impact that he still considers Chicagoans to be the best registers of national attitudes and problems and the city itself to be the most "concentrated social laboratory of American life."[1]

The Chicago he knew as a boy, he once wrote, did not flood him with "the great waves of hope that Dreiser felt when he was young and first came to the city," but the hope was there for the finding. As Farrell has stated in his letter to Stanley Pargellis, July 25, 1949, Chicago's sharp contrasts of grandeur and misery nourished "a very dynamic life . . . in which there was growth, change, a tremendous drama of human destiny being hammered out." As a young man Farrell learned that the dynamism was fed by such thinkers as Professors Veblen, Dewey, and Mead of the University of Chicago. By the late 1920's, Farrell knew both Chicagos, the stagnant and the dynamic; and their interaction sent him on his way—a personal rebel against a stifling business culture, a militant advocate of social reform, and a writer.

The literary climate of the 1920's intensified Farrell's need for self-expression and rebellion. He valued H. L. Mencken and Sinclair Lewis, for example, as liberating voices speaking for truth and enlightenment, whether in literature or life. As he fairly lunged toward his future career, he had every reason to value the attainment of truth and enlightenment in his own writing through the honest representation of reality as he had experienced it.

Resemblances may be found between Farrell's writing and that of some eighteenth- and nineteenth-century Realists, American and foreign; but Farrell himself has typically—and soundly—linked his Realism to the literary tendency that he has called the American "cultural nationalism" of the twentieth century. Authors in that movement, he believed—as he told Thomas H. Uzzell on March 1, 1939—wrote of the American social realities they knew most intimately, such as the conflicts arising from the "many old world cultural patterns that have been refashioned in terms of life on this continent." Farrell added in this letter that the writer as "cultural nationalist" was likely to view his material from "critical and realistic perspectives." Dreiser, Anderson, Lewis, and Edgar Lee Masters, he noted, gave impetus to the tendency —one that Farrell himself advanced by exploring the cultural patterns of his own neighborhood and, in the process, extending the reach of Realistic fiction in this era.

Viewed in a larger context, Farrell's fiction clearly falls within the classical line of the novel's development: the tradition of critical Realism. He has sought his meanings in actual experience by representing characters in a definite time and place and in complex relationship to other individuals. He has shown their destinies being shaped by the milieu and the period, by their particular roles in society, and by their qualities of character. In being faithful to the cultural and material environments that shape his characters' spirits, Farrell has avoided reliance upon the transcendent or upon the legendary and mythological—the resources of the symbolic novelist. The symbols immanent in Farrell's writing intensify and focus the meaning of the concrete reality portrayed, but they remain organic with it. Nor do they emerge as semi-independent allegories.

Similarly, Farrell's narrative techniques and his non-poetic language are appropriate to his concentration upon reality as it actually is felt by specific individuals in a particular time and place, usually, but by no means invariably, Chicago and New York neighborhoods of the 1920's and 1930's. Technique and language are used to communicate and to objectify the empirically experienced reality, whether manifested as "environment" or as subjective impression, reverie and dream. In short, Farrell has employed the classic means of the Realist in combination with modern themes to highlight important human problems and to provide, through the carefully developed destinies of his characters, a vision of humanity and of some alternatives open to men in this world.

The literary means Farrell has employed are deeply appropriate to his ontology, which is naturalistic, empirical, secular. "By naturalism," Farrell has written, "I mean that whatever happens in this world must ultimately be explainable in terms of events in this world. I assume or believe that all events are explainable in terms of natural origins rather than of extranatural or supernatural origins" (*RAF*, 150). Philosophically, Farrell's world is not one of essence but one of relationship, process, tendency, change, emergence, and time leading onward to death. Most of his fiction, sometimes thought of as a formless overflow of memory, may reasonably be regarded as a selection of experience that imaginatively embodies the world as process, adhering to the logic of life as he conceives it. For his fiction is faithful to the concreteness and the flow of events, to psychological relativism, and to natural causation. Farrell's ambiguous and shifting status early in life, so deeply felt, was an ideal ground for the development of this philosophy, just as this philosophy formulates the assumptions underlying what and how he has written.

One of Farrell's distinctions is the literary form he evolved—most successfully in the Studs Lonigan and the Danny O'Neill series. In those works, the particular blend of a bold architectural structure, an objective narrative method, and a style attuned to the idiom of his characters and to the quality of their experience was his own creation, one designed to express the life he knew intimately in Chicago. Nevertheless, his avid consumption of books that began in 1925 inevitably shaped his thinking and writing.

Among the writers of fiction who influenced him in the 1920's, a few deserve particular mention. To Farrell, Theodore Dreiser was a symbol of integrity, an uncompromising fighter against great odds who broke fresh ground for later writers. Farrell's style and method, and indeed the effects he creates, have little resemblance to Dreiser's, nor could Farrell accept Dreiser's gloomy philosophy; but he valued the older man's depth of feeling and his broad sympathy and respect for humanity. Moreover, Dreiser's picture of Chicago and of boyhood was meaningful to Farrell, who imaginatively identified Dreiser's Clyde Griffiths with boys he had known, and Carrie and Jennie with his aunts. Sherwood Anderson's fiction, even more than Dreiser's, gave Farrell confidence in his boyhood as material for literature, in part because Farrell intimately identified with Anderson's deviate characters who affected him deeply. Their inner life, Farrell recognized, was presented as meaningful and important. Anderson's ordinary, inarticulate persons, like Farrell's Studs and Danny, craved understanding; they were beset by frustrations that spawned lonely, cramped selves, and even aggression.

From Hemingway's fiction Farrell gained some suggestions for stories and, more important, an electric impression of immediacy, of the intensely vernacular, as though the action were taking place next door in America even when it was occurring in Europe. Hemingway's use of dialogue for narration was a revelation to Farrell, and his style helped Farrell discard an adolescent subjectivity and a constant striving for metaphors apparent in his 1927 college writing. James Joyce's fiction, which also helped Farrell acquire objectivity in his prose, presented dramatic action through the interior monologue, the dream, and the staccato-like progression of snapshot episodes like that in the party scene ending *The Young Manhood of Studs Lonigan.* Joyce as Irish rebel and spoiled priest was significant to Farrell, for Joyce's exploration of the themes of self-discovery and of the artist's developing consciousness struck home.

Numerous philosophers, social scientists, and others redirected Farrell's thinking during the 1920's and thereby opened up per-

spectives within his writing. In 1927 Farrell, somewhat like
Bernard Clare, briefly acted the part of a Nietzschean rebel—
self-assertive and superior, a Dionysian truth-seeker and destroyer, the archenemy of Christianity and all shackling delusions
—even though Dreiser's attitudes of sympathy and acceptance
served as a counterpoise in his total consciousness at the time.
Today it is possible to say that Nietzsche's influence pervades
Farrell's writing. It merges importantly into the total ethical
and social thrust of his fiction, for it helped give form to the individualistic, revolutionary strain native to Farrell.

Even more significant in Farrell's development were the American pragmatists William James, John Dewey, and George H.
Mead. (Farrell's intimate knowledge of the writing of these men,
especially Dewey's and Mead's, and his close alliance with their
intellectual tradition, are evident in *Dialogue on John Dewey*
[1959].) Separate studies have examined this relationship, and
here it is enough to indicate the profundity of Farrell's indebted-
ness. Pragmatist thought shaped his social values and his concept
of man in freedom and in bondage. It enlarged his understanding of social and individual growth. Especially Dewey and Mead
have had much to do with Farrell's stand in ethics, esthetics, and
metaphysics. And because Farrell absorbed their concepts of
time, emergence, reverie, habit, and the interaction of the self
with other selves and the environment, their influence may be
seen as a kind of stance toward experience that he developed, or
even as an organizing principle affecting the style and structure
of his fiction.

Thorstein Veblen's ideas excited Farrell in the 1920's. Veblen's
theory of business enterprise clarified Farrell's understanding of
the economic system and of his experience within it as a lowly
service-station attendant. Veblen helped Farrell see that an
acquisitive society and a standardized industrial order often
thwart man's best instincts and stunt personal creativity. Similarly Charles Beard's *An Economic Interpretation of the Consti-
tution of the United States* shaped Farrell's view of historical
cause and effect, and John Maynard Keynes' *The Economic Consequences of the Peace* revealed to Farrell a new, unhappy vista
of a violent future. Just as unhappy was the longer vista ending
in universal death presented in Bertrand Russell's "A Free Man's
Worship," but Russell taught Farrell the value of stoicism and

the dignity of human striving for a better life on earth. Walter Pater also spoke to Farrell about the proper use of time and consciousness. As Farrell moved from the 1920's into the 1930's, the influences of Sigmund Freud and of Karl Marx, Leon Trotsky, and other revolutionists became more pronounced, although not so basic as that of the pragmatists.

Contemporary novelists have taken many directions other than those followed or pioneered by Farrell, yet he has had considerable effect upon later writers. Frederick J. Hoffman and Willard Thorp have indicated that his influence has been pervasive and persistent, like that of Dreiser and Hemingway. In Blanche H. Gelfant's penetrating study *The American City Novel*, she has concluded that Farrell's pioneering development of the ecological novel and its appropriate techniques has been absorbed by other novelists to a remarkable degree. It seems likely that Farrell has influenced, in one way or another and among others, the work of Willard Motley, Daniel Fuchs, Leonard Bishop, Meyer Levin, Sam Ross, J. F. Powers, Nelson Algren, Richard Wright, Hal Ellson, James Jones, Herman Wouk, and Norman Mailer.

II *Estimates*

Farrell's initial advantage as a writer was his thorough possession of an urban, Irish Catholic world. His fiction shows a talent for exploring the sources of his growth in that world. In doing so, Farrell brings his Chicago into focus; he creates his larger self—his famous "South Side" in its spatial, temporal, cultural, and emotional dimensions—by including in his picture family, society, and cultural process that extends over half a century. Farrell explores this past, so crucially important to him, with great objective validity, and he extends the picture to other parts of America and the world. The writing remains intensely personal—a deep strength—if only because its subject, the education of Americans, is rooted in Farrell's early predicament and in his accomplishment, just as many of his characters are imagined versions of the possibilities and actualities of his experience.

Farrell also writes out of other strengths. A man of passion and reason, he is an utterly serious truth-teller. His insights are penetrating; his intelligence, quick and strong. His consciousness is involved with broad social questions and with the mysteries of the self. He understands spiritual poverty, its causes, and what should replace it. Since he has moved freely about the world, his experience with men, both sophisticated and simple, has been broad and unsheltered. Well read in world literature and other fields, he has thought deeply about the ends and means of his craft. With great integrity he has kept to his vision of life which, as Horace Gregory has well said, is elemental, direct, humane, and moral. And Farrell is still writing.

Farrell's novels and tales are informed with a rich blend of attitudes and perspectives in addition to that supplied by his philosophic Naturalism. His Humanism recognizes man's idealism as well as his shabbiness; it assumes, therefore, man's capacity for reason and dignity as well as for degradation. His critical Realism is friendly to modern pragmatism and to reformist social thought. Where values are concerned, his fiction says to us that the only real ends are earthly consequences and that in human society consequences are men and women who are affected for better or worse by their culture. As he once said in New Delhi, "We must strive to create a society in which everybody can have the best possible chance to realize themselves . . . what is important is *not* what happens to us after we die, but . . . how we act . . . to create a free society."[2] Farrell's writing takes account of the irrational and the evil within both the individual and society, and it affirms the possibility of making a better world by acting with courage, reason, and love. His faith is in the human spirit. If we believe, with Kenneth Burke, "that the visions that give purpose and unity to historic movements are in essence religious,"[3] then the breadth and nonsectarian quality of Farrell's religious imagination are apparent. Here as elsewhere, Farrell's technique contributes to his effects. Part of what it creates through its empirical idiom is the living presence of the Satanic and the Promethean in man's consciousness—although neither Farrell nor his characters would be likely to so phrase the matter.

Farrell's fiction also says that elemental emotions impel men and women toward self-fulfillment or self-deception. At its heart is an ethics of self-development that is also displayed in his rise from "plebeian" origins and in his stubborn independence of mind. This ethics is a kind of Emersonian individualism without the supernatural aura. It asserts the possibility of radical self-improvement through the right and the will to grow. He has written: "Man is my concern . . . the dream that each and all have the opportunity to rise to the full stature of their potential humanity."[4] Farrell is a philosophic Naturalist—although his Catholic imagination is still alive—who simultaneously sees life in the context of death and who affirms with utter seriousness the values of the Enlightenment.

A Universe of Time, Farrell's work in progress, is too incomplete to judge. As it grows, it evidently will continue to be compatible in themes and patterns of experience with his earlier work; but it may also develop new techniques suitable to its own purpose and it may give fresh emphases to Farrell's interpretation of the past. For many years Farrell has believed that the emergence of novelty in the present constantly changes the meaning of the past; and for a novelist, as he stated in a letter to Dr. Noah Fabricant on June 14, 1939, this means "that the past has to be put into a new system," for "new pasts are always rising behind us." Whatever may be the potential of *A Universe of Time,* its published portions do not as yet make the strong and unified impact of either *Studs Lonigan* or the O'Neill-O'Flaherty series.

The two cycles centering on Studs and Danny represent to date Farrell's major contribution to American literature. They are large-scale, complementary works that express more thoroughly and more passionately than his other writing the central experience of his life: his emergence from a condition of cultural and spiritual deprivation. *Studs Lonigan* shows the final tragic consequence of the deprivation as well as the processes of disintegration. The O'Neill-O'Flaherty books do not take us so far in the opposite direction, for Danny's emergence does not have the finality of Studs's death. When we last see Danny in the pentalogy, he has only begun to practice the new insights and the freedom he has won. Yet the direction he is taking, its potential meaning, and the outcome he desires are indicated with sufficient clarity. Like the earlier trilogy, the later cycle convincingly dramatizes in detail the human processes it portrays.

As I hope this book has indicated, Farrell's power as a writer of fiction is likely to appear under various guises in many works. But in *Studs Lonigan* and the O'Neill-O'Flaherty series his art is at its consistent best. There, with impressive success, he has brought together his main literary strengths: an elemental insight —getting at the roots of things; a consuming imagination that greedily transforms experience into a sustained illusion of life; the ability to evoke, from that illusion, moral and social meanings strikingly relevant to contemporary civilization; the power of realistic characterization evident in most of his work, applied intensively to twelve or fifteen major characters, both men and women, and extensively to hundreds of others; a pronounced architectural skill in putting together massive fictional structures derived from firsthand experience; and the suitability of those structures and of his style to his subject.

Some parts of the foregoing estimate agree with the evaluations of others, including Joseph Warren Beach, Blanche H. Gelfant, and Henry H. Dyer, whose detailed and well-documented study of Farrell's artistry is as yet unpublished; but it contradicts the judgments of still others. In 1932 two early reviews of *Young Lonigan* in the New York *Times* and in the *Saturday Review of Literature* denied artistry and imagination to Farrell and thus, at the very beginning of his public career as novelist, set a pattern of criticism frequently repeated since then. Very possibly Farrell has been attacked in print more often than any other American author of this century, for his critical Realism has a remarkable capacity for treading on toes and offending specialized sensibilities. It is safe to say that, over the years, Marxists, New Humanists, censors and guardians of public morals, Catholic and Christian apologists, and many professors, including New Critics and myth and symbol critics, have not looked kindly on him.

Needless to say, Farrell's predominantly hostile critics have indicated some genuine weaknesses in his art. But the denunciations by Stalinists and moralistic critics of the 1930's and 1940's are little more today than historical curiosities. Likewise, much past academic criticism of Farrell is irrelevant or mistaken; often it is excessively vehement and easily falls into blanket condemnation. A surprising amount of it conveys less of substance than an incredible air of condescension.

In preceding pages I have tried to suggest my disagreement with some major adverse criticisms of Farrell's writing. First is the objection that Farrell lies outside the Christian-Humanistic tradition and that, lacking a religio-mythic imagination, he reinforces what is inhuman and mindless in the modern world, when the times cry out for the artist to renovate the human spirit. A second, very common criticism is that the meaning emerging from Farrell's fiction is the doctrine of "pessimistic determinism" that rigidly denies free will and moral responsibility. A third criticism is directed at the method rather than the meaning of Farrell's Naturalism. It states that his writing, lacking personal involvement or imagination, is equivalent to stenography, newspaper reporting, undiscriminating documentation, verbal photography, and field-telephone messages, none of which yields anything beyond case studies, sociology, or the environment. A fourth criticism is that in method and intention Farrell imitates one or more masters such as Dreiser or Zola (Farrell first read Zola in 1936 and 1937). Fifth, critics have seen his fiction as stylistically inept, structurally weak, and deficient in characterization. Finally, Farrell's artistry, along with that of Daniel Defoe and other "committed realists," has been dismissed as inconsequential for having failed to develop the techniques of symbolist fiction or, indeed, *any* techniques worthy the name. Such authors, it is said, "deny the resources of art for the sake of life."[5]

Farrell's work, like that of other writers, is uneven from book to book and exhibits both weaknesses and strengths, the weaknesses sometimes being the defects of the strengths. For example, it may be said that at times Farrell depends too exclusively on dialogue for characterization, yet that technique dramatically reveals the mentality behind the words and thus carries and verifies the thematic indictment of what city life does to people. His writing can be doggedly repetitive and wordy, but again it is often so for thematic purposes—just as Walt Whitman, Henry James, and William Faulkner can be repetitive and wordy in their ways to achieve their effects. Such flaws of his style, if that is what they are, are in any case minor compared to its virtues in his best work: its over-all thematic suitability, its expressive adaptability to the speech patterns of many characters, its frequent attainment of a natural eloquence.

Traits of Farrell's style are closely tied to his method of letting life speak (particularly in early works) or of making the written word a fit vehicle for the characters' language and patterns of consciousness and thus, as Farrell stated in his letter to James Henle, July 14, 1934, "never violating in any important sense, the facts of their life, never compounding the attitudes of different characters into one." This theory of objectivity, with its self-imposed restrictions of viewpoint and language, limits the effects Farrell can achieve, as he has recognized; for it forecloses other narrative approaches to his material. Also it discounts brevity and foreshortening, and it may even reduce the sharpness and solidity with which Farrell represents the external world. Yet the method is the source of memorable artistic effects often uniquely handled. It is the right method for his intention because it embodies his meaning and because it works to disclose it. Similarly, the one-dimensional quality of some of Farrell's characters—who are nonetheless thoroughly believable—is right for their supporting roles and their thematic significance. Nor should these characters blind us to Farrell's undoubted power to create more rounded characters of great vitality.

The personal and ultimately self-centered quality of Farrell's art, although essential to its accomplishments, helps to explain some of its limitations. His shaking the sack of reality—his intimate reality—until it is empty bespeaks an admirable desire to master what is genuinely his own and to record it all. But this effort sometimes hampers control and selectivity, always a problem for Farrell, who once stated in a letter to James Henle, July 28, 1942: "What is called the imagination . . . is not completely subject to control; you can't use it as you use a machine; at times, it seems as if one's imagination were a race horse one is riding." This same self-centered quality occasionally makes for writing that lacks sufficient esthetic distance. Sometimes, too, as with the character Bernard Carr, a preoccupation with the personal quest diminishes the specification of external reality—absorbs it inward into the self—at the very time its full presence is needed to give added significance to the quest.

Moreover, Farrell's imagination is most vitally engaged with his pre-University of Chicago life, that experience of the nerve-ends and emotions that absorbed him for years. He best creates the wounded and confused boy, the aspiring or rebellious young man, the adult grotesque—in short, those very human personalities who are deeply involved with their family and their severely limited culture. In his diary for July 16, 1945, Farrell recognized his difficulty in creating mature, complex adults. Yet the grand design of his fiction, as well as the dynamics of his social philosophy that values awareness, breadth of experience, and reason, calls for an equally convincing picture of men and women who have emerged into larger worlds. As Robert Gorham Davis has cogently argued, Farrell's fiction does not do complete justice to what is rich and creative in human consciousness, Farrell's included.

In other words, Farrell has not realized the full potential in his vision. But his vision is large and single, and step by step he has created a single world of ample proportions. His cycles of novels with his other fiction approximate a sequence, a rarity in American literature. At its best, the American past he creates is deeply authentic as art and as social history, like Faulkner's South. Farrell's re-created and recorded past is especially meaningful to us because, through its rich details of urban manners, it shows the heavy cost exacted of people and institutions by the modern city. His characters' lives expose social process; time slowly brings change, and the making of personality and the formation of society merge. His Lonigans, O'Flahertys, and O'Neills are deeply immersed in their time and place—interesting contrasts to Hemingway's disengaged Americans—and his work is exceptional in our fiction for the number of its living characters. The contrast between their often blind groping for a better future and the grimness of their present, flowing inevitably out of their past, is a subject with tragic power.

Notes and References

Chapter One

1. "Some Notes on My MIS-Education at a Catholic High School." Manuscript, University of Pennsylvania Library.

2. Farrell stated: "I used to be a very intense critic of parochial schools. I was wrong. I'm not a religious person, but I learned four things and absorbed four things: (1) that truth is possible, it's possible to think of the world in terms of order; (2) I was never told a lie; I was given a conception of the meaning of the truth as important; (3) I got a sense there was something before me and something after me . . . and that I was living in a continuity where there was depth of experience and where there was an idea of greatness and grandeur and also of mystery and reality—where you face tragedy, you face yourself. You ask yourself if you sin or not. That can have the effect of making you see rather realistically. (4) I got the idea that there are things so important in this world that it's your duty to die for them if necessary, and that the values are more important than you.

"I had those feelings and they are, as best as I could put them, in my work." From "A Novelist's Reflections on Writing and His World," *Catholic Messenger* (October 31, 1963), p. 5, as transcribed from a lecture of September 24, 1963.

3. *Oriflamme,* January-February, 1922, p. 30.

4. *Reflections at Fifty and Other Essays* (New York, 1954), p. 130; hereafter cited in text as *RAF*.

5. In a letter dated March 17, 1932, to James Henle, Farrell wrote that Samuel Putnam "was the first person known at all to read any parts of *Young Lonigan* and like it. In fact it was that playground scene [in *Young Lonigan*] which interested him. I sent it to *This Quarter* in 1930 while I was writing the book and he was on the magazine and fought vainly with Titus to have it printed." A letter from Putnam to Farrell, April 23, 1930, bears out Farrell's remarks.

6. As editor of the *New Review,* Samuel Putnam often turned to his associate editor Ezra Pound for an opinion. He wrote to Farrell on March 12, 1931, of Pound's enthusiastic liking for Farrell's writings, and in an undated letter to Farrell quoted Pound: "So long as

Farrel [*sic*] is getting pubd that seems to me to fill the bill." Pound liked both "Jewboy" and "The Scarecrow" and advised printing them together: "Effect cumulative, and shows that a new writer is here" (undated letter to Farrell).

7. *A Note on Literary Criticism* (New York, 1936), p. 11; hereafter cited in text as *Note*.

8. *The League of Frightened Philistines and Other Papers* (New York, 1945), p. 105; hereafter cited in text as *League*.

9. *The Name Is Fogarty* (New York, 1950), p. 25; hereafter cited in text as *Name*.

Chapter Two

1. In an undated letter to Victor Weybright, Farrell explained "how *Studs* became three": "I planned *Studs* as one volume and began from the end, backward—from death backward. This was June, 1929. . . . I wrote most of what became Volumes I and II between June, 1929 and February, 1931. It was too much for one book—for the reader to take. I made Section One a novel and called it *Young Lonigan*.

"In June, 1931, when I lived in Sceaux, France . . . I put aside the manuscript and wrote *Gas House McGinty*. My plan was to do a second Studs book and end with his death. I got the idea of a sick and dying fantasy scene of the Day of Judgment as the way to describe Studs's death. And I wrote the dream chapter of *Gas House McGinty* as a preparation for this planned scene.

"In 1934, when I was completing *The Young Manhood of Studs Lonigan*, my intention was to end with my Judgment Day fantasy. However, I saw that the novel would take nothing after the Party scene, except at a cost of weakening the book. That's how *Studs* became three. I decided for Volume III to write a fantasy of the Day of Judgment. In the fall of 1934 I started *Judgment Day*. My plan was to do one chapter, writing about the father, and use this to set up the fantasy. The book evolved itself. I invented from day to day. Finally, I wrote the fantasy. But I only used a page or so of it. I kept the rest."

Most of the fantasy was burned in the December, 1946, fire in Farrell's New York City apartment. Farrell reassembled some surviving sheets and published them as "Fragments from the unpublished death fantasy sequence of 'Judgment Day,'" *Tri-Quarterly*, I (Winter, 1965), 127-38. Newton Berry has written an informative preface to the fantasy sequence in *Tri-Quarterly*.

2. As early as October, 1933, Farrell was thinking about doing five other books: a critical volume re-evaluating twenty to thirty American novelists from James to Hemingway and Faulkner; two novels con-

cerning New York literary life; the novel which became *Ellen Rogers;* a novel about six or more families in a Chicago apartment building. The last work was intended to criticize the way Americans live and to do "what Dos Passos has always attempted, but to my mind failed in accomplishing." He believed it would make greater demands upon his technical facility and his imagination than any books he had yet written. (Letter to James Henle, October 8, 1933.)

3. From a deleted portion of the manuscript of the Introduction to *Studs Lonigan: A Trilogy,* Modern Library edition (New York, 1938).

4. *The Young Manhood of Studs Lonigan,* p. 59. All quotations from *Young Lonigan, The Young Manhood of Studs Lonigan,* and *Judgment Day* are from *Studs Lonigan: A Trilogy,* the 1938 Modern Library edition. Hereafter the three novels will be cited in the text as *YL, YMSL,* and *JD,* respectively. The trilogy will be cited as *Studs Lonigan.*

5. Introduction to *Studs Lonigan,* p. xiv.

6. Farrell's comments on the originals of his characters, as in the letter cited, frequently employ their fictional names—a practice followed in the text at this point. His comments suggest that, in his opinion, his characters as a rule have been modeled after one or more persons he has known, without, however, being literal portrayals. Thus he has written that the characterization of Mr. Lonigan drew upon Farrell's uncle Tom Daly; that of Mrs. Lonigan, upon his mother and grandmother; that of Catherine Banahan, upon Dorothy Farrell and a girl whom he knew in Saratoga Springs. See Farrell's letter of January 15, 1946, to James Henle, and Farrell's diary, July 16, 1945.

7. In attemping to explain the psychological origins of *Studs Lonigan* in his letter to James Henle dated January 15, 1946, Farrell assumed the existence of a boyhood antipathy toward his father and his elder brother Earl and connected it to his feelings for Studs and Red Kelly. In letters of August 13 and 15, 1961, to me, he rejected his assumption as "too limited and non-inclusive," believing it was based on no evidence other than "a subjective feeling I had in 1946."

8. In the revised version of "Studs" originally printed in *Guillotine Party and Other Stories* (New York, 1935), the narrator comments about Studs: "I grew up contemptuous of him and the others . . ." (p. 300). The original version in *This Quarter* (July-August-September, 1930) more truly indicates Farrell's change in attitude: "I grew contemptuous of him, and the others. . . ."

9. The quotations from "Studs" in this paragraph and the next are from the revised version in *Guillotine Party and Other Stories,* pp. 294-305.

10. Compare Farrell's statement ending his essay "Reflections at Fifty": "I, too, spit into the face of time, even though I am aware that this is merely a symbolic expression of a mood: Time slowly transfigures me just as it transfigures all of us. There is no security in an insecure world. There is no final home on a planet where we are homeless children. In different ways, we find a sense of security, of permanence, or of home—for a while. To me, impermanence renders everything good and beautiful all the more rare. It stimulates my ambition and it strengthens the stoicism which is at the root of my outlook about experience." *Reflections at Fifty and Other Essays* (New York, 1954), p. 65.

Chapter Three

1. Untitled Notebook, probably 1929 and 1930, p. 25. University of Pennsylvania Library.
2. "James Farrell on James Farrell," *New Republic*, CIII (1940), 596.
3. From a deleted portion of the manuscript of the Introduction to *Studs Lonigan*.
4. *Human Nature and Conduct* (New York, 1922), p. 64.
5. John Crowe Ransom, "Reconstructed but Unregenerate," *I'll Take My Stand* (New York, 1930), p. 10.
6. Ransom, p. 17.
7. George H. Mead, "The Genesis of the Self and Social Control," *International Journal of Ethics*, XXXV (1924), 268.

Chapter Four

1. These five books, all published by Vanguard Press, will be cited in the text as *World, Star, Son, Days*, and *Face*, respectively.
2. Untitled typescript by Farrell, p. 1; hereafter cited in text as Typescript A.
3. *The Life Adventurous and Other Stories* (New York, 1947), pp. 281-313. Hereafter cited in text as *Life*.
4. Untitled typescript [B] by Farrell, p. 3.
5. "Origin of 'Helen, I Love You,'" MS dated May 11, 1951, University of Pennsylvania Library.
6. *Ibid.*
7. *Ibid.*
8. *Boarding House Blues* (New York, 1961), p. 151; hereafter cited in text as *BHB*.

Chapter Six

1. These three novels, all published by Vanguard Press, will be cited in the text as *Clare, Road,* and *Yet,* respectively.

Chapter Seven

1. *Gas-House McGinty* (New York, 1933), p. 153; hereafter cited in text as *McGinty.*
2. Henle responded that presumably Farrell's intention was similar to that of John Howard Lawson in his play "Processional," only "with the scene limited to an express company unit rather than a mining town" (letter to Farrell, August 3, 1931).
3. See Farrell's letters to James Henle, April 30 and May 18, 1941.
4. *New Year's Eve/1929* (New York, 1967), p. 51; hereafter cited in text as *NYE.*
5. From two reviews of *Can All This Grandeur Perish? and Other Stories:* Alfred Kazin, "The Bitter Bread of James T. Farrell," New York *Herald Tribune Books,* May 16, 1937, p. 6; S. L. Solon, "Mr. Farrell's Short Stories," *Modern Monthly,* X (August, 1937), 16.
6. *The League of Frightened Philistines and Other Papers* (New York, 1945), p. 140.
7. "Preface," *The Short Stories of James T. Farrell* (New York, 1937), p. xlviii.
8. *Calico Shoes and Other Stories* (New York, 1934), pp. 176-77.
9. *No Star Is Lost* (New York, 1938), pp. 252-53.

Chapter Eight

1. "The Mowbray Family" in *When Boyhood Dreams Come True* (New York, 1946), p. 276.
2. Hereafter cited as *CP* in documenting quotations from poems in the text.
3. Briefer publications that are part of *A Universe of Time* are: the tales "Native's Return," "On the Appian Way," "Forty-Five Minutes Out of Life," "The Lady and the Masters of History," "When Three Is Not a Triangle," and "Ray Taite"; the poem "On a Day of Inclement Weather Over One Hundred Years Ago"; and the short articles "Woodrow Wilson Remembered" and "Question Asked in a Hospital." In addition, Farrell has published excerpts from later novels in the series, "The Vast Present" and "A Universe of Time."
4. "When Time Was Young," p. 21, undated typescript by Farrell.
5. *Ibid.,* p. 17.
6. *The Silence of History* (New York, 1963), p. 362; hereafter cited in text as *Silence.*

7. *Lonely for the Future* (New York, 1966), p. 204; hereafter cited in text as *Lonely*.

8. Max Stirner, *The Ego and His Own* (New York, 1918), p. 246.

9. *When Time Was Born* (New York, 1966), p. 23; hereafter cited in text as *Born*.

10. *What Time Collects* (New York, 1964), p. 118; hereafter cited in text as *WTC*.

11. *A Brand New Life* (New York, 1968), p. 181; hereafter cited in text as *BNL*.

12. Farrell's 1966 tale "When Three Is Not a Triangle" reveals that Anne and George lived together five or six weeks. Anne returns to Valley City when George starts hitchhiking East with Eddie Ryan and an ex-professor named Elkin. See *Today*, XXII (October, 1966), 25-28.

13. *Judith* (Athens, Ohio, 1969), p. 20.

14. *Invisible Swords* is scheduled for publication in 1971 by Doubleday. I am grateful to Mr. Farrell for having permitted me to read the novel in manuscript (May, 1970) and to discuss it in print before publication and sale. Under the circumstances, I have thought it best to confine my remarks largely to a description of content and an indication of theme and structure. Documentation in the text refers to manuscript page numbers.

John Stephen Farrell was born in September, 1947, to Mr. Farrell and Hortense Alden Farrell. On August 30, 1949, he was placed in Letchworth Village. That same month Farrell wrote "Little Tommy," an early first-person version of the present Chapter III of *Invisible Swords*, the episode in which Bill Martin, waiting in the hospital, receives word of Billy's birth and foot deformity. In a letter of May 11, 1954, to James Henle from Paris, Farrell revealed that he had completed nineteen sections of his novel, then called *Moonlight on the Mountain*, and was writing six to ten pages a day. His writing flowed best, he continued, "when there is no strain, when I feel that I am letting life speak for itself." He described the book as sad and having "a growing intensity," a work that troubled him "because the unhappiest part of the past lays raw and open in my mind." The book represented to him "one strain" in his writing: "what I shall call naked tragedy," and specifically "the biological tragedy of man which is not reversible." Farrell continued to work on his manuscript in 1954, returned to it recurrently through the late 1950's and 1960's, and on June 3, 1965, in a letter to me, stated that it was "finally revised."

Chapter Nine

1. "Chicago and American Culture," *Thought,* XIII (November 25, 1961), 14.

2. "The Twentieth Century American Novel," June 8, 1956.

3. Kenneth Burke, "Change of Identity," *New Republic,* LXXXIII (June 19, 1935), 171.

4. "And Now after a Stalemate—What?," *Crisis* (Chicago, 1964), pp. 69-70.

5. Mark Schorer, "Technique as Discovery," *Forms of Modern Fiction,* ed. William Van O'Connor (Minneapolis, 1948), p. 29.

Selected Bibliography

PRIMARY SOURCES

Only Farrell's major books are listed. For his many uncollected writings and a few separate publications of collected pieces, see the bibliographies mentioned below.

1. Novels and Novellas

Young Lonigan: A Boyhood in Chicago Streets. New York: Vanguard Press, 1932.
Gas-House McGinty. New York: Vanguard Press, 1933.
The Young Manhood of Studs Lonigan. New York: Vanguard Press, 1934.
Judgment Day. New York: Vanguard Press, 1935.
Studs Lonigan: A Trilogy. New York: Vanguard Press, 1935. *(Young Lonigan, The Young Manhood of Studs Lonigan,* and *Judgment Day.)*
A World I Never Made. New York: Vanguard Press, 1936.
No Star Is Lost. New York: Vanguard Press, 1938.
Tommy Gallagher's Crusade. New York: Vanguard Press, 1939.
Father and Son. New York: Vanguard Press, 1940.
Ellen Rogers. New York: Vanguard Press, 1941.
My Days of Anger. New York: Vanguard Press, 1943.
Bernard Clare. New York: Vanguard Press, 1946.
The Road Between. New York: Vanguard Press, 1949.
This Man and This Woman. New York: Vanguard Press, 1951.
Yet Other Waters. New York: Vanguard Press, 1952.
The Face of Time. New York: Vanguard Press, 1953.
Boarding House Blues. New York: Paperback Library, 1961.
The Silence of History. New York: Doubleday, 1963.
What Time Collects. New York: Doubleday, 1964.
Lonely for the Future. New York: Doubleday, 1966.
New Year's Eve/1929. New York: The Smith, 1967.
A Brand New Life. New York: Doubleday, 1968.
Judith. Athens, Ohio: Duane Schneider Press, 1969.
Invisible Swords. New York: Doubleday, planned for 1971.

2. Collected Short Stories

Calico Shoes and Other Stories. New York: Vanguard Press, 1934.
Guillotine Party and Other Stories. New York: Vanguard Press, 1935.
Can All This Grandeur Perish? and Other Stories. New York: Vanguard Press, 1937.
The Short Stories of James T. Farrell. New York: Vanguard Press, 1937. (Reprints the preceding three volumes.)
$1,000 a Week and Other Stories. New York: Vanguard Press, 1942.
To Whom It May Concern and Other Stories. New York: Vanguard Press, 1944.
When Boyhood Dreams Come True. New York: Vanguard Press, 1946.
The Life Adventurous and Other Stories. New York: Vanguard Press, 1947.
An American Dream Girl. New York: Vanguard Press, 1950.
French Girls Are Vicious and Other Stories. New York: Vanguard Press, 1955.
An Omnibus of Short Stories. New York: Vanguard Press, 1957. (Reprints *$1,000 a Week and Other Stories, To Whom It May Concern and Other Stories, The Life Adventurous and Other Stories.*)
A Dangerous Woman and Other Stories. New York: Vanguard Press, 1957.
Side Street and Other Stories. New York: Paperback Library, 1961.
Sound of a City. New York: Paperback Library, 1962.
Childhood Is Not Forever. New York: Doubleday, 1969.
Judith and Other Stories. New York: Doubleday, planned for 1971.

3. Poetry and Prose Poem

The Collected Poems of James T. Farrell. New York: Fleet Publishing Corporation, 1965.
When Time Was Born. New York: The Smith, 1966.

4. Criticism, Collected Essays, and Other Prose

A Note on Literary Criticism. New York: Vanguard Press, 1936.
The League of Frightened Philistines and Other Papers. New York: Vanguard Press, 1945.
Literature and Morality. New York: Vanguard Press, 1947.
The Name Is Fogarty; Private Papers on Public Matters. New York: Vanguard Press, 1950.
Reflections at Fifty and Other Essays. New York: Vanguard Press, 1954.
My Baseball Diary. New York: A. S. Barnes Co., 1957.
It Has Come to Pass. New York: Theodor Herzl Press, 1958.

Dialogue on John Dewey, ed. Corliss Lamont. New York: Horizon Press, 1959. Farrell one of eleven contributors to this discussion.

SECONDARY SOURCES

1. A. Bibliography

BRANCH, EDGAR M. *A Bibliography of James T. Farrell's Writings, 1921-1957.* Philadelphia: University of Pennsylvania Press, 1959.
————. "A Supplement to the Bibliography of James T. Farrell's Writings," *American Book Collector,* XI (Summer, 1961), 42-48.
————. "Bibliography of James T. Farrell: A Supplement," *American Book Collector,* XVII (May, 1967), 9-19.
WESTLAKE, NEDA M. "The James T. Farrell Collection at the University of Pennsylvania," *American Book Collector,* XI (Summer, 1961), 21-23. Describes the Collection.

2. Critical Studies

Listed below are selected general studies of Farrell's work and a few specialized studies particularly useful for supplementing this book.

BEACH, JOSEPH WARREN. "James T. Farrell: Tragedy of the Poolroom Loafer" and "James T. Farrell: The Plight of the Children." *American Fiction, 1920-1940.* New York: Macmillan, 1941. Sound estimate of Farrell's work through 1940.
BRANCH, EDGAR M. "American Writer in the Twenties: James T. Farrell and the University of Chicago," *American Book Collector,* XI (Summer, 1961), 25-32. Farrell's college days.
————. "Freedom and Determinism in James T. Farrell's Fiction." *Essays on Determinism in American Literature,* Ed. Sydney J. Krause. Kent, Ohio: Kent State University Press, 1964. Influence of American pragmatists on Farrell.
CURLEY, THOMAS F. "Catholic Novels and American Culture," *Commentary,* XXXVI (July, 1963), 34-42. Farrell as "the most representative of the American 'Catholic' Novelists."
DYER, HENRY HOPPER. "James T. Farrell's Studs Lonigan and Danny O'Neill Novels." Unpublished dissertation, University of Pennsylvania, 1965. Perceptive study of Farrell's artistry in the two cycles.
FROHOCK, WILLIAM M. "James Farrell: The Precise Content," *The Novel of Violence in America, 1920-1950.* Second edition. Dallas: Southern Methodist University Press, 1958. Farrell as a documentary novelist.
GELFANT, BLANCHE H. "James T. Farrell: The Ecological Novel." *The American City Novel.* Norman: University of Oklahoma Press, 1954. Major study of Farrell's fiction through 1953.

182   JAMES T. FARRELL

LICKSBERG, CHARLES I. "The Criticism of James T. Farrell," *South-west Review*, XXXV (Summer, 1950), 189-96. Emphasizes Farrell's polemics against doctrinaire Marxist esthetics.

GRATTAN, C. HARTLEY. "James T. Farrell: Moralist," *Harper's*, CCIX (October, 1954), 93-98. Excellent about Farrell's moral thought.

GREGORY, HORACE. "James T. Farrell: Beyond the Provinces of Art," *New World Writing*, V (April, 1954), 52-65. Evaluation of Farrell as a major Realistic novelist.

KAZIN, ALFRED. *On Native Grounds.* New York: Reynal and Hitchcock, 1942. Farrell as a left-wing Depression Naturalist.

LOVETT, ROBERT MORSS. "James T. Farrell," *English Journal*, V (May, 1937), 347-54. Reprinted as "Introduction" to *The Short Stories of James T. Farrell*. New York: Vanguard Press, 1937. Early penetrating study of Farrell's art.

LYNCH, WILLIAM JAMES. "The Theory and Practice of the Literary Criticism of James T. Farrell." Unpublished dissertation, University of Pennsylvania, 1966. Helpful exploration of "the nexus between [Farrell's] critical theory, practical criticism, and creative literature."

MITCHELL, RICHARD. "*Studs Lonigan:* Research in Morality," *Centennial Review,* VI (Spring, 1962), 202-14. Excellent study of Dewey's influence on *Studs Lonigan* regarded as research in morality.

O'MALLEY, FRANK. "James T. Farrell: Two Twilight Images." *Fifty Years of the American Novel: A Christian Appraisal.* Harold C. Gardiner, ed. New York: Scribner's, 1951. Farrell's images of civilization and the Catholic Church.

REITER, IRENE MORRIS. "A Study of James T. Farrell's Short Stories and Their Relation to His Longer Fiction." Unpublished dissertation, University of Pennsylvania, 1964. Useful analysis and appraisal of Farrell's short stories.

WALCUTT, CHARLES C. "James T. Farrell: Aspects of Telling the Whole Truth." *American Literary Naturalism, A Divided Stream.* Minneapolis: University of Minnesota Press, 1956. Farrell's major cycles related to stages in the development of Naturalist theory.

Index

Farrell, Helen (sister), 18
Farrell, Hortense Alden (wife), 15, 30, 124, 135, 177
Farrell, James (grandfather), 17
Farrell, James Francis (father), 17, 18, 174
Farrell, James Thomas: literary plan, 15-16; ancestry, 16-18; boyhood, 18-21; grammar school education, 19-21; on Catholic education, 21, 172; high school education, 21-22; literary influences on, 22-23, 26, 161, 163; university education, 22-24; in Paris, 24-26; New York City residence, 24, 26-30; at Yaddo, 27; relations to Communists, 28-29, 30, 33, 34; journalism, 30-32; theory of literature and literary criticism, 32-33; social criticism, 33-34; unity of his fiction, 34-35; Naturalistic philosophy, 43, 166-67, 175; attitude toward Catholic Church, 49; Realism and Naturalism of, 161-62, 169; intellectual influences on, 161-65; pragmatism of, 164, 166; literary influence of, 165; ethical views, 166-67; critics on, 168-69; literary strengths and weaknesses, 167-71
WRITINGS OF:
"Accident" (short story), 78
"After the Sun Has Risen" (short story), 128
"An American Student in Paris" (short story), 133
"And Now after a Stalemate—What? (essay), 178
"Angela" (short story), 78
"Autumn Afternoon" (short story), 77, 128, 132
"Baseball Is Changing" (editorial), 31
Bernard Clare (novel), 24, 105-15 *passim*, 109-10
Bernard Carr trilogy *(Bernard Clare, The Road Between, Yet Other Waters)*, 82, 105-15; ori-

gin and writing of, 105-07; Bernard's development, 107-13; Communist theme in, 107-13; use of setting, 114-15; 117, 125, 135, 139, 141, 170
"Blisters" (short story), 129
Boarding House Blues (novel), 83, 84, 124-26, 134, 145, 147
"Boyhood" (short story), 77, 118
"Boys and Girls" (short story; deletion from *Young Lonigan*), 128
A Brand New Life (novel), 139, 151-53
"Calico Shoes" (short story), 127
Calico Shoes and Other Stories, 26, 36, 127, 128, 130
"A Casual Incident" (short story), 77, 131
Chamber of Horrors (discarded title for early collection of tales), 26
"Chicago and American Culture" (essay), 178
Childhood Is Not Forever (short stories), 127-28
"Clyde" (short story), 78
The Collected Poems of James T. Farrell, 135-39
"Comedy Cop" (short story), 133
"The Control of TV" (editorial), 31
Danny O'Neill pentalogy *(The Face of Time, A World I Never Made, No Star Is Lost, Father and Son, My Days of Anger)*, 34-35, 36-37, 61, 74-104; origin and writing of, 74-80; time span, 75; centrality in Farrell's work, 80-84; major characters, 84-87; Chicago setting, 87-89; Danny's development, 91-100; methods of characterization, 100-03; 117, 141, 142, 162, 167
"Dewey in Mexico" (essay), 32
Dialogue on John Dewey (discussion by Farrell and ten others), 164

University of Chicago, Farrell at-
tends, 23-24; Farrell's campus
writing, 30, 118, 127, 160; and
Danny O'Neill, 74, 75, 78, 98-
99, 126; 87, 99; and Eddie Ryan,
142-44
Uzzell, Thomas H., 161

Vanzetti, Bartolomeo, 109, 110
Veblen, Thorstein, Farrell reads, 23;
influences Danny O'Neill, 74, 98;
161; influences Farrell, 164; *The
Theory of Business Enterprise*, 74
Villon, François, 136

Walsh, Ed, 19, 95
Walter, Father Leo J., O.C.C., 22
Weatherwax, Clara, Farrell's review
of *Marching! Marching!* 28

Webb, John Edgar, 136
West, Nathanael, 27
Weybright, Victor, 173
Whitman, Walt, and *When Time
Was Born*, 147; 169; "Song of
Myself," 147
Willingham, Calder, 106
Wilson, Woodrow, 37, 176
Witwer, H. C., influences Farrell,
22
Wolfe, Thomas, Farrell reads, 26;
114
Wouk, Herman, 165
Wright, Richard, 165

Yaddo, Farrell lives at, 27

Zola, Émile, 169